Better Homes and Gardens®

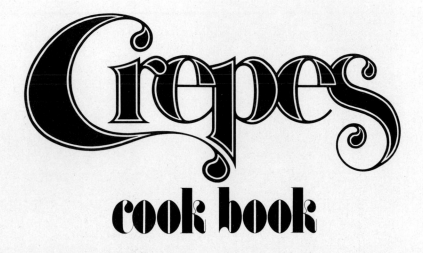

Crepes cook book

Above: *Peachy Pecan Crepes* is a refreshing blend of crepes, pecans, peaches, and orange liqueur. (See recipe, page 69.)

On Cover: Recipes are *Asparagus-Ham Roll-Ups, Shrimp Chow Mein Dinner,* and *Strawberry Shortcake Stacks.* (See Index.)

BETTER HOMES AND GARDENS BOOKS

Editorial Director: Don Dooley
Art Director: John Berg   Asst. Art Director: Randall Yontz
Production and Copy Chief: Lawrence D. Clayton
Food Editor: Doris Eby
Senior Associate Food Editor: Nancy Morton
Senior Food Writer: Sharyl Heiken
Associate Editors: Rosemary C. Hutchinson, Sandra Granseth,
    Diane Nelson, Elizabeth Strait
Assistant Editor: Flora Szatkowski
Graphic Designers: Harijs Priekulis, Sheryl Veenschoten, Faith Berven

Contents

Our seal assures you that every recipe in the
Crepes Cook Book is endorsed by the Better Homes
and Gardens Test Kitchen. Each recipe is
tested for appeal, practicality, and deliciousness.

International specialties translate easily into tasty fillings
for crepes. Here, *Ratatouille-Filled Crepes* provide an extra
use for a flavorful favorite. (See recipe on page 62.)

Create a crepe

Elegant restaurants have long had a monopoly on crepes. Not any longer, though! Now, it's your turn to discover just how easy these tender, thin pancakes with delicious fillings and savory sauces are to make and serve. In no time at all you'll be duplicating any of the crepe masterpieces a famous chef can prepare, and much, much more.

The delicate pancake batter is a smooth mixture of flour, eggs, milk, salt, and cooking oil or melted butter. Dessert types usually contain a small amount of sugar, too. You also can concoct intriguing variations with additional ingredients such as cornmeal, whole wheat flour, or cocoa that complement special fillings. These versions, together with basic crepe recipes, begin on page 11.

Is it crêpes or crepes?

Fortunately, it's no more difficult to pronounce crepes than it is to make them. The word crêpes (rhymes with preps) is French and sounds just right with Crêpes Suzette. But thin pancakes are wraparounds for morsels of meat or sweet in a good many other countries, so you can call them crepes (rhymes with drapes), if you prefer.

What equipment is needed?

For hundreds of years crepes have been made in six-inch skillets—this is still the utensil many people prefer. (Actually, you can use a griddle or electric frypan, but the round shape of the crepe is more difficult to achieve.) However, the inverted crepe pan, such as the one pictured on page 8, deserves credit for generating much of today's interest in crepes. This piece of equipment has literally turned the art of crepemaking upside down.

Both pans make thin, tender crepes (all but a few recipes in this book adapt to either type of pan). To make crepes in a skillet you pour and cook the batter on the inside of the pan. To make crepes with an inverted pan you dip the bottom of the pan in the batter and cook it on the outside surface. Some skillets will make crepes either inside or on the outside of the pan. Housewares departments everywhere feature electric and non-electric models of all these versions.

When do you serve crepes?

Anytime! Crepe creations fit a multitude of serving situations. One time, make them small for party appetizers. Another time, plan two regulars as a satisfying entrée. Choose a flaming dessert as grand finale for a dinner, or simply stack crepes with sliced fruit between the layers as a snack. Serve them wrapped around ice cream or layered with cream cheese. Heat the crepes in an oven, in a chafing dish, or with a microwave oven.

How to make crepes

Each little pancake is made from about two tablespoons of batter cooked in a small skillet (see how-to drawings 1-3 at the right) or on an inverted crepe pan (see how-to drawings 4-7 on page 8). A little practice with either piece of equipment will make you an expert. However, if you should have any difficulty, refer to the tip box on page 39 to find the easy solution to the problem. And, don't worry if there's an occasional break or if a bubble leaves a tiny hole while the crepe is cooking. Simply patch it with a little of the batter and continue cooking a few seconds until the patch is set.

You'll notice that there is no need to flip a crepe if you make a point of spooning the filling on the unbrowned side. This way when you roll up the crepe, the unbrowned side will be well hidden in the middle. Likewise, when you stack several crepes, be sure to layer all but the first one with unbrowned side down.

Some crepe fans insist that the secret to tender, no-stick crepes is to let the batter stand one or two hours before use. Better Homes and Gardens Test Kitchen experience shows you can skip this step when preparing all of the crepe batters in this book. Granted, the batter is important, but success really depends on a seasoned skillet (or pan with nonstick surface) that is heated to the right temperature. Seasoning directions come with most pans that require it, but if you need more information about seasoning a pan, check the tip box on page 32.

Fillings and toppings

Crepe combinations come in unbelievable variety. In fact, you can chop or slice almost any cooked meat, vegetable, or fruit and roll it inside a crepe. This applies to leftovers, too. (You'll find the chart on page 93 particularly handy. It lists the crepe recipes throughout the book that take advantage of leftovers.)

Recipes in this book specify the type of crepe, tell how to make filling and sauce, and give easy-to-follow directions for assembling and serving the finished dish. Later, you'll have ideas of your own and want to change the filling or put together new combinations. The basic filling and sauce recipes beginning on page 17 give you a head start.

As you page through the recipes, you will see that not all of them have both a filling and a sauce. Sometimes, especially in the dessert category, crepes are just folded and heated or flamed in a fabulous sauce. Harvey Wallbanger Crepes and Classic Crêpes Suzette (see recipes, pages 74 and 82) are two tasty examples. Another, Swedish Pancake Roll-Ups (see recipe, page 48), has so much goodness going for it inside the crepes that a sauce isn't needed.

Crepes in a skillet: (1) Holding heated skillet with one hand, pour 2 tablespoons of crepe batter into pan. Quickly rotate pan so that batter covers bottom in a thin, even layer. Return skillet to heat and cook 45 to 60 seconds.

(2) When crepe is lightly browned on bottom*, invert pan and let crepe drop out of pan onto paper toweling. You may need a small spatula to get it started. Let each crepe cool completely before stacking with 2 layers of waxed paper in between.

Electric skillet crepe pan: (3) This appliance has a heat regulator to maintain cooking temperature. Check owner's manual for settings and timings. Follow the same quick rotating motion when pouring batter into this type of pan.

*Note: No need to brown the second side of the crepe. Spoon filling on unbrowned side and roll or fold as desired.

(more information on page 10)

7

Inverted pan crepes

Crepes on an inverted pan: Prepare cooking surface according to manufacturer's directions. Pour batter into shallow bowl or pie plate. (4) Dip heated crepe pan, rounded side down, into the batter. Hold a few seconds to be sure surface is covered with batter. Quickly turn right side up.

(5) Set electric model on the countertop and cook crepes according to manufacturer's directions. (6) Return the non-electric model to range top and cook crepes 45 to 60 seconds.

(7) When crepe is lightly browned,* hold pan over paper towel and loosen crepe with spatula. (If crepe pan has a nonstick coating, be sure to use a nylon or other nonmetal utensil.) Let each crepe cool completely before stacking with 2 layers of waxed paper in between.

Note: No need to brown crepe on second side. Spoon filling on unbrowned side and roll or fold as desired.

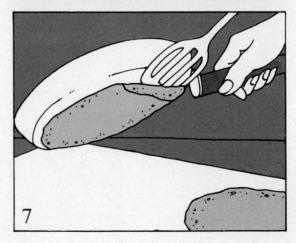

Lapped fold: (8) Spoon filling along center of unbrowned side of crepe. Fold two opposite edges so they overlap atop filling. Follow recipe directions as to whether fold is placed up or down.

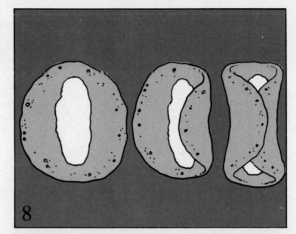

Quarter fold: (9) Spoon filling in center of unbrowned side of crepe. Fold crepe in half and then in half again, forming a triangle.

Stacked crepes: (10) Place single crepe, browned side down, on a plate. Spread filling over surface. Lay another crepe, browned side up, on top of the first. Repeat last step with desired number of crepes, all browned side up. Cut in wedges to serve.

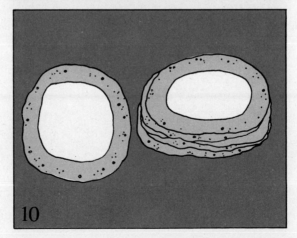

(continued on next page)

Packet fold: (11) Spoon filling in center of unbrowned side of crepe. Fold two opposite edges so they overlap atop filling. Fold remaining edges toward center to form a square packet. Place seam side down on serving plate or in baking dish according to directions for the particular dish involved.

Crepe shapes

Most crepes are folded or stacked in somewhat traditional ways. The four versions on pages 9 and 10 are the best known. A fifth, not shown, is the rolled crepe, which, as the name implies, is simply spread with a filling and rolled up like a jelly roll.

In most cases the folds are interchangeable. For convenience, all of the recipes in this book will include a traditional or preferred fold for each dish. But don't let this stop you. You can present a favorite recipe in a different form each time you prepare it.

You don't necessarily have to roll, fold, or stack crepes, though. You can bake them over custard cups and fill the resulting crepe cup with a luscious Shrimp Chow Mein Dinner, as shown on the cover. Or, snip them into strips, fry in deep fat, and incorporate into a tempting nibble snack such as Peanut-Crepe Nibble Mix (see recipe, page 57). If you have a few crepes left over, cut them in strips and drop them into hot broth for a quick homemade noodle soup.

Prepare crepes ahead

No rule says that you have to make crepes the same day you plan to use them. In fact, you can do them a day, a week, or two months in advance. Or, make them without a special occasion in mind and store them in the freezer to whisk out for impromptu company. Just remember that any filling mixture that will freeze alone can be rolled in a crepe and frozen complete. Details on freezing crepes either plain or with a filling appear in the tip box on page 12.

Basic crepes

Basic Main Dish Crepes

1 cup all-purpose flour
1½ cups milk
2 eggs

1 tablespoon cooking oil
¼ teaspoon salt

In a bowl combine flour, milk, eggs, oil, and salt; beat with a rotary beater until blended. Heat a lightly greased 6-inch skillet. Remove from heat; spoon in about 2 tablespoons batter. Lift and tilt skillet to spread batter evenly. Return to heat; brown on one side only. (*Or* cook on inverted crepe pan, see page 8.) To remove, invert pan over paper toweling; remove crepe. Repeat with remaining batter to make 16 to 18 crepes, greasing skillet occasionally.

Calorie Counter's Crepes

These crepes have only 34 calories each—look for other low-calorie recipes in the book—

1 cup all-purpose flour
1½ cups skim milk

1 egg
¼ teaspoon salt

In bowl combine flour, milk, egg, and salt; beat with a rotary beater till blended. Heat a lightly greased 6-inch skillet. Remove from heat; spoon in about 2 tablespoons batter. Lift and tilt skillet to spread batter. Return to heat; brown on one side only. (*Or* cook on inverted crepe pan, see page 8.) Invert pan over paper toweling. Remove crepe. Repeat to make about 18 crepes, greasing skillet occasionally.

Tangy Buttermilk Crepes

¾ cup all-purpose flour
1 cup buttermilk
½ cup milk
2 eggs

1 tablespoon cooking oil
1 teaspoon sugar
¼ teaspoon salt

In bowl combine flour, buttermilk, milk, eggs, oil, sugar, and salt; beat with rotary beater till blended. Heat a lightly greased 6-inch skillet. Remove from heat; spoon in 2 tablespoons batter. Lift and tilt skillet to spread batter. Return to heat; brown on one side only. (*Or* cook on inverted crepe pan, see page 8.) Invert pan over paper toweling; remove crepe. Repeat to make 16 to 18, greasing skillet occasionally.

How to Freeze Crepes

Unfilled crepes freeze well, so while you have your crepe pan or skillet out, do up an extra batch and store them in your freezer. Just make a stack, alternating each crepe with two layers of waxed paper. (The waxed paper makes crepes easy to separate.) Then, overwrap the stack in a moisture-vaporproof bag. Before freezing protect the crepes by placing the bag in a glass or plastic container. Keep crepes frozen no longer than two to four months. To use remove as many crepes as you need, then reseal the bag and return crepes to the freezer. Let crepes thaw at room temperature about one hour before using.

For filled crepes, place them on a greased baking sheet without touching; freeze uncovered. When frozen, remove and seal in a moisture-vaporproof bag. Then place crepes in a glass or plastic container for protection. Return to freezer. Most meat fillings and fruit fillings freeze well, but avoid freezing potato, mayonnaise, cooked egg white, raw vegetable, and cream fillings. Use filled crepes within two months. Thaw frozen crepes before heating.

Fluffy All-Purpose Crepes

3 *eggs, separated*
¾ *cup all-purpose flour*
1 *cup milk*

2 *tablespoons cooking oil*
1 *teaspoon sugar*
⅛ *teaspoon salt*

Beat egg whites till stiff peaks form; set aside. In bowl combine flour, egg yolks, milk, oil, sugar, and salt; beat with rotary beater till blended. Fold in egg whites. Heat a lightly greased 6-inch skillet. Remove from heat. Spoon in 2 tablespoons batter; lift and tilt skillet to spread batter. Return to heat; brown on one side only. (*Or* cook on inverted crepe pan, see page 8.) Invert over paper toweling; remove crepe. Repeat with remaining batter to make 20, greasing skillet often.

Yellow Cornmeal Crepes

⅓ *cup all-purpose flour*
1½ *cups milk*
⅔ *cup yellow cornmeal*

2 *eggs*
1 *tablespoon cooking oil*
¼ *teaspoon salt*

In bowl combine flour, milk, cornmeal, eggs, oil, and salt; beat with rotary beater till blended. Heat a lightly greased 6-inch skillet (*don't use an inverted crepe pan*). Remove from heat. Spoon in about 2 tablespoons batter; lift and tilt skillet to spread batter evenly. Return to heat; brown one side only. Invert pan over paper toweling; remove crepe. Repeat to make 16 to 18 crepes, greasing pan occasionally. Stir batter frequently to keep cornmeal from settling. Don't freeze these, as they crumble when frozen.

Parmesan Cheese Crepes

1 *cup all-purpose flour*
1½ *cups milk*
2 *eggs*

¼ *cup grated parmesan cheese*
1 *tablespoon cooking oil*

In bowl beat flour, milk, eggs, parmesan, and oil with rotary beater till blended. Heat a greased 6-inch skillet. Remove from heat. Add 2 tablespoons batter; lift and tilt to spread batter. Return to heat; brown one side. (*Or* cook on inverted crepe pan, see page 8.) Invert over paper toweling; remove crepe. Repeat to make 18, greasing skillet.

Whole Wheat Crepes

In bowl combine 1 cup whole wheat flour, 1½ cups milk, 2 eggs, 1 table-spoon cooking oil, and ¼ teaspoon salt; beat with rotary beater till blended. Heat a lightly greased 6-inch skillet. Remove from heat. Spoon in about 2 tablespoons batter; lift and tilt skillet to spread batter. Return to heat; brown on one side. (*Or* cook on inverted crepe pan, see page 8.) Invert pan over paper toweling; remove crepe. Repeat with remaining batter to make 16 to 18 crepes, greasing skillet occasionally.

Feathery Sour Cream Crepes

In bowl combine 1 cup all-purpose flour, 1½ cups milk, ½ cup dairy sour cream, 2 eggs, 2 tablespoons sugar, and ⅛ teaspoon salt; beat with rotary beater till blended. Heat a lightly greased 6-inch skillet. Remove from heat. Spoon in about 2 tablespoons batter; lift and tilt skillet to spread batter. Return to heat; brown on one side only. (*Or* cook on inverted crepe pan, see page 8.) Invert pan over paper toweling; remove crepe. Repeat to make 20 to 22 crepes, greasing skillet occasionally.

Pancake Mix Crepes

In bowl combine 1 cup packaged pancake mix, 1¼ cups milk, 2 eggs, 1 tablespoon sugar, and 1 tablespoon cooking oil; beat with rotary beater till blended. Heat a lightly greased 6-inch skillet. Remove from heat. Spoon in about 1½ tablespoons batter; lift and tilt skillet to spread batter evenly. Return to heat; brown on one side only. (*Or* cook on inverted crepe pan, see page 8.) Invert pan over paper toweling; remove crepe. Repeat to make about 24 crepes, greasing skillet occasionally.

Blender Dessert Crepes

In blender container add ½ cup all-purpose flour, ¾ cup milk, 1 egg, 1 egg yolk, 1 tablespoon sugar, 1 tablespoon cooking oil, and ⅛ teaspoon salt. Cover and blend till smooth, about 45 seconds. Heat a greased 6-inch skillet. Remove from heat. Add 2 tablespoons batter; lift and tilt skillet to spread batter. Return to heat; brown on one side. (*Or* cook on inverted crepe pan, see page 8.) Invert over paper toweling; remove crepe. Repeat to make 10 to 12 crepes, greasing skillet.

Basic Dessert Crepes

1 cup all-purpose flour
1½ cups milk
2 eggs

2 tablespoons sugar
1 tablespoon cooking oil
⅛ teaspoon salt

In bowl combine flour, milk, eggs, sugar, oil, and salt; beat with a rotary beater till blended. Heat a lightly greased 6-inch skillet. Remove from heat. Spoon in 2 tablespoons batter; lift and tilt skillet to spread batter. Return to heat; brown on one side. (*Or* cook on inverted crepe pan, see page 8.) Invert pan over paper toweling; remove crepe. Repeat to make 16 to 18 crepes, greasing skillet.

Chocolate Dessert Crepes

If you prefer, substitute 1¼ cups chocolate milk for the milk and cocoa powder—

1 cup all-purpose flour
1½ cups milk
⅓ cup pre-sweetened instant
    cocoa powder

2 eggs
1 tablespoon cooking oil
1 teaspoon vanilla

Combine all ingredients; beat with rotary beater till blended. Heat a greased 6-inch skillet. Remove from heat. Add 2 tablespoons batter; lift and tilt skillet to spread batter. Return to heat; brown on one side. (*Or* cook with inverted crepe pan, see page 8.) Invert over paper toweling; remove crepe. Repeat to make 16 to 18, greasing skillet.

Spicy Dessert Crepes

1 cup all-purpose flour
1⅓ cups milk
2 eggs
2 tablespoons brown sugar
2 tablespoons cooking oil

1 tablespoon light molasses
½ teaspoon ground cinnamon
¼ teaspoon ground ginger
⅛ teaspoon ground nutmeg

Combine all ingredients; beat with rotary beater till blended. Heat a greased 6-inch skillet. Remove from heat. Add 2 tablespoons batter; lift and tilt skillet to spread batter. Return to heat; brown on one side. (*Or* cook on inverted crepe pan, see recipe page 8.) Invert over paper toweling; remove crepe. Repeat to make 16 to 18, greasing skillet.

Lemon Dessert Crepes

1 *cup all-purpose flour*
1½ *cups milk*
2 *eggs*

2 *tablespoons sugar*
1 *tablespoon cooking oil*
1½ *teaspoons grated lemon peel*

Mix all ingredients and ⅛ teaspoon salt; beat with rotary beater. Heat a lightly greased 6-inch skillet. Remove from heat. Add 2 tablespoons batter; lift and tilt skillet to spread. Return to heat; brown one side. (*Or* cook on inverted crepe pan, see page 8.) Invert over paper toweling; remove crepe. Repeat to make 16 to 18, greasing skillet.

Coffee Dessert Crepes

½ *cup all-purpose flour*
¾ *cup milk*
1 *egg*

1½ *teaspoons sugar*
1 *teaspoon instant coffee*
 crystals

Combine all ingredients and dash salt; beat with rotary beater till blended. Heat a lightly greased 6-inch skillet. Remove from heat. Add 2 tablespoons batter; lift and tilt skillet to spread. Return to heat; brown on one side. (*Or* cook on inverted crepe pan, see page 8.) Remove crepe over paper toweling; repeat to make 8 crepes, greasing skillet.

Crepe Chips or Crepe Noodles

Make Basic Main Dish Crepes (see page 11). With a sharp knife, cut each crepe into 8 wedges to make chips *or* into ¼-inch strips (about 3 inches long) to make noodles. In heavy medium saucepan or skillet at least 3 inches deep, heat 1 inch cooking oil to 375°. Place a layer of chips or noodles in a deep fat basket; dip into hot fat. Fry till crisp, 1 to 1½ minutes, stirring once. Drain well. Use as a snack.

Oven-Baked Crepe Cups

Invert custard cup on a baking sheet. Generously grease outside of custard cup. Place one Basic Main Dish Crepe (see page 11), browned side up, atop cup. Press crepe lightly to fit cup. Repeat to make desired number. Bake at 375° till crisp, 20 to 22 minutes.

Basic sauces and fillings

Creamy Velouté Sauce

2 *tablespoons butter* or
    margarine
3 *tablespoons all-purpose flour*

1 *cup chicken broth*
⅓ *cup light cream*

In saucepan melt butter; blend in flour. Add broth and cream all at once. Cook and stir till thickened and bubbly. Makes 1½ cups.

Golden Béchamel Sauce

¼ *cup finely chopped onion*
1 *tablespoon butter* or
    margarine
1 *tablespoon all-purpose flour*

½ *teaspoon salt*
    Dash white pepper
1¾ *cups milk*
3 *beaten egg yolks*

Cook onion in butter till tender. Blend in flour, salt, and pepper. Add milk all at once. Cook and stir till thickened and bubbly. Stir half the hot mixture into egg yolks; return to pan. Cook and stir over low heat 2 to 3 minutes. Do not overcook. Makes 2¼ cups.

Blender Hollandaise Sauce

In blender container add 3 egg yolks, 2 tablespoons lemon juice, and dash cayenne. Cover; quickly turn blender on and off. Heat ½ cup butter *or* margarine till melted and almost boiling. Turn blender on high speed; slowly pour in butter, blending till thick, about 30 seconds. Heat over *warm, not hot* water till ready to serve. Makes 1 cup.

Mornay Sauce with Wine

3 *tablespoons butter* or
    margarine
3 *tablespoons all-purpose flour*
¼ *teaspoon ground nutmeg*

1 *cup light cream*
¼ *cup dry white wine*
⅓ *cup shredded process Swiss*
    cheese

In saucepan melt butter; blend in flour, nutmeg, ¾ teaspoon salt, and dash pepper. Add cream all at once. Cook and stir till thickened and bubbly. Stir in wine. Add cheese; stir till melted. Makes 1½ cups.

Classic Béarnaise Sauce

3 tablespoons tarragon vinegar
1 teaspoon finely chopped
   shallots or green onion
4 whole black peppercorns,
   crushed
   Dried tarragon

Dried chervil
4 egg yolks
½ cup butter, softened
1 teaspoon snipped fresh
   tarragon or ¼ teaspoon
   dried tarragon, crushed

In saucepan mix vinegar, shallots, peppercorns, and a little dried tarragon and chervil; simmer till reduced to half. Strain; add 1 tablespoon cold water. Beat egg yolks in top of double boiler (not over water). Slowly add herb liquid. Add a few tablespoons butter to egg yolks; place over *hot, not boiling water.* Cook and stir till butter melts and sauce begins to thicken. Continue adding remaining butter, a few tablespoons at a time, and stirring till sauce is like thick cream. Remove from heat. Salt to taste; add fresh tarragon. Makes 1 cup.

Vanilla Custard Sauce

4 beaten egg yolks
¼ cup sugar
   Dash salt

2 cups milk, scalded and
   slightly cooled
1 teaspoon vanilla

In a heavy saucepan combine egg yolks, sugar, and salt. Gradually stir in scalded milk. Cook and stir over low heat till mixture coats a metal spoon. Remove from heat; cool pan at once by setting in cold water. Stir for a minute or two. Stir in vanilla. Chill. Makes 2 cups sauce.

Daffodil Lemon Sauce

½ cup sugar
4 teaspoons cornstarch
   Dash ground nutmeg
2 beaten egg yolks

2 tablespoons butter or
   margarine
½ teaspoon grated lemon peel
2 tablespoons lemon juice

In saucepan mix sugar, cornstarch, nutmeg, and dash salt. Gradually stir in 1 cup water. Cook and stir over low heat till thickened. Stir *half* the hot mixture into egg yolks; return to pan. Cook and stir 1 minute. Remove from heat; blend in remaining ingredients. Makes 1 cup.

Regal Chocolate Sauce

Mix 1 cup sugar, 1 cup water, and ½ cup light corn syrup; cook to soft ball stage (*or* till candy thermometer registers 236°). Remove from heat; add three 1-ounce squares unsweetened chocolate, cut up. Stir till melted. Add 1 teaspoon vanilla. Blend in ½ cup evaporated milk. Makes 1¾ cups.

Vanilla Cream Filling

⅓ cup sugar
3 tablespoons all-purpose flour
¼ teaspoon salt
1¼ cups milk

1 beaten egg
1 tablespoon butter or
   margarine
1 teaspoon vanilla

Combine sugar, flour, and salt. Slowly add milk; mix well. Cook and stir over medium heat till thickened and bubbly; cook and stir 2 minutes more. Gradually stir *half* the hot mixture into egg; return to pan. Cook and stir till just boiling. Stir in butter and vanilla; cover surface with clear plastic wrap. Cool (do not stir). Makes 1½ cups.

Chocolate Filling: Prepare Vanilla Cream Filling, increasing sugar to ½ cup. Add one 1-ounce square unsweetened chocolate, cut up, with milk.

Butterscotch Filling: Prepare Vanilla Cream Filling, substituting packed brown sugar for granulated sugar. Increase butter to 2 tablespoons.

Glossy Lemon Filling

¾ cup sugar
2 tablespoons cornstarch
  Dash salt
¾ cup cold water

2 beaten egg yolks
1 teaspoon grated lemon peel
3 tablespoons lemon juice
1 tablespoon butter

In heavy saucepan combine sugar, cornstarch, and salt; gradually add water. Stir in egg yolks, lemon peel, and lemon juice. Cook and stir over medium heat till thickened and bubbly. Boil 1 minute; remove from heat. Stir in butter. Cool (do not stir). Makes 1⅓ cups.

Lime Filling: Prepare Glossy Lemon Filling, substituting 1 teaspoon grated lime peel and 3 tablespoons lime juice for lemon peel and juice. Add 1 drop green food coloring with butter, if desired.

Orange Filling: Prepare Glossy Lemon Filling, substituting ¾ cup orange juice for the water. Omit lemon peel and lemon juice.

Inviting Crepe Entrées

The next time you need a new idea for a meal—brunch, lunch, dinner, or a late-night snack, serve any of the wide assortment of main dish crepes you'll find in this section. The brunch or luncheon idea shown here features *Brunch Crepes with Apple Rings* (see recipe, page 34) and *High-Top Shrimp Crepes* (see recipe, page 32). Round out the meal by including a favorite fruit juice such as apple cider and coffee or milk.

Poultry

Elegant Crepes Divan

1 10¾-ounce can condensed cream
   of chicken soup
1 teaspoon Worcestershire sauce
   Dash ground nutmeg
1 8-ounce package frozen cut
   asparagus

2 cups chopped cooked turkey
12 Tangy Buttermilk Crepes
   (see recipe, page 11)
½ cup grated parmesan cheese
½ cup whipping cream
½ cup mayonnaise

For sauce: Blend together soup, Worcestershire, and nutmeg.
For filling: Cook asparagus according to package directions; drain. Combine asparagus and turkey. Blend in ¼ *cup* of the sauce.
To assemble: Spoon about ¼ cup filling along center of unbrowned side of each crepe. Fold crepes in half. Place crepes in a 13x9x2-inch baking dish. Spoon remaining sauce over crepes. Top with *half* of the cheese. Bake, covered, at 375° till heated through, 25 to 30 minutes. Whip cream till soft peaks form; fold in mayonnaise. Spread over crepes. Top with remaining cheese. Broil 3 to 4 inches from heat till golden, 2 to 3 minutes. Makes 6 servings.

Chicken 'n' Broccoli Crepes

6 tablespoons butter or
   margarine
6 tablespoons all-purpose flour
   Dash salt
3 cups milk
½ cup shredded sharp American
   cheese (2 ounces)
¼ cup dry white wine

1 2½-ounce jar sliced mushrooms,
   drained
1 10-ounce package frozen
   chopped broccoli
2 cups finely chopped cooked
   chicken
12 Basic Main Dish Crepes (see
   recipe, page 11)

For sauce: In a medium saucepan melt butter. Blend in flour and salt. Add milk all at once. Cook, stirring constantly, till thickened and bubbly. Stir in cheese and wine till cheese melts. Remove ½ *cup* of the sauce; set aside. Stir mushrooms into remaining sauce.
For filling: Cook broccoli according to package directions; drain. Combine drained broccoli, chicken, and the ½ cup reserved sauce.
To assemble: Spread ¼ cup filling over unbrowned side of crepe, leaving ¼-inch rim around edge. Roll up crepe. Place seam side down in skillet or chafing dish. Repeat with remaining crepes. Drizzle sauce over crepes. Cook, covered, over low heat till bubbly. Makes 6 servings.

Chicken 'n' Broccoli Crepes served from a chafing dish make an elegant meal easy to manage. Using this stylish pan allows you to spend less time in the kitchen—more with your guests.

Curried Turkey Stack-Ups

Yellow Cornmeal Crepes batter
(see recipe, page 13)
¼ *cup chopped onion*
¼ *cup chopped green pepper*
1 *small clove garlic, minced*
2 *tablespoons butter* or
  margarine
2 *cups chopped cooked turkey*
1 *16-ounce can tomatoes, cut up*
2 *tablespoons dried currants*
2 *tablespoons snipped parsley*
1 *to 2 teaspoons curry powder*
1 *teaspoon salt*
⅛ *teaspoon pepper*
  Dash ground mace
2 *tablespoons cold water*
1 *tablespoon cornstarch*
½ *cup shredded American cheese*
  (2 ounces)

For crepes: Using 1 tablespoon batter for each, prepare 24 crepes by spooning batter onto hot lightly greased 6-inch skillet, spreading batter with back of spoon to make a 4-inch circle. Brown on one side only.

For sauce: In saucepan cook onion, green pepper, and garlic in butter *or* margarine till tender but not brown. Stir in turkey, undrained tomatoes, currants, parsley, curry powder, salt, pepper, and mace. Cook, stirring occasionally, till heated through, about 10 minutes. Blend cold water into cornstarch; stir into turkey mixture. Cook, stirring constantly, till mixture is thickened and bubbly.

To assemble: Arrange 4 crepes in a single layer, browned side down, in 13x9-x2-inch baking dish. Spread 2 tablespoons sauce over each crepe. Repeat layering crepes (*browned side up*) and sauce 4 more times, ending with sauce. Add another crepe to each stack, making four stacks of 6 crepes each. Sprinkle *each* stack with *2 tablespoons* of the cheese. Bake, uncovered, at 350° till heated through, 15 to 20 minutes. Makes 4 servings.

Cooking Tips for Crepes

When a recipe calls for 2 cups chopped or cubed cooked chicken, use leftover chicken or buy two whole chicken breasts (about 10 ounces each). Bring chicken breasts and 2 cups salted water or chicken broth to boiling. Reduce heat. Cover and simmer till chicken is tender, about 20 minutes. Remove chicken and cool slightly. Discard skin and bones; cut up meat.

If you're planning to use the cooked chicken later, wrap meat loosely (or place in a covered dish) and refrigerate promptly. Use within one to two days. For longer storage, wrap meat tightly in moisture-vapor-proof material, such as heavy foil or freezer bags. Seal, label, and freeze up to one month.

Chicken Crepes with Rum Sauce

4 whole medium chicken breasts,
  skinned, boned, halved
  lengthwise, and
  cut in strips
2 tablespoons cooking oil
1 cup chopped onion
1 clove garlic, minced
1 16-ounce can tomatoes, cut up
2 tablespoons lime juice
1 teaspoon salt

½ teaspoon dried oregano,
  crushed
⅛ teaspoon pepper
¼ cup raisins
1 8¼-ounce can pineapple
  chunks
⅓ cup rum
2 tablespoons all-purpose flour
10 to 12 Basic Main Dish Crepes
  (see recipe, page 11)

For sauce: In skillet brown the chicken lightly in oil. Add onion and garlic; cook until onion is tender. Drain tomatoes; reserve liquid. Set tomatoes aside. Add reserved liquid, lime juice, salt, oregano, and pepper to chicken. Cover and simmer for 10 minutes. Add tomatoes and raisins. Simmer, covered, for 15 minutes. Remove chicken; set aside. Cut up pineapple; add to sauce with rum. Blend ¼ cup cold water into flour; stir into sauce. Cook and stir till thickened and bubbly.

To assemble: Divide chicken among crepes, placing strips along center of unbrowned side of each crepe. Fold two opposite edges of each crepe so they overlap atop filling. Place in skillet with tomato mixture. Spoon sauce over. Cover and heat through. Makes 5 or 6 servings.

Cranberry-Turkey Crepes

2 cups chopped cooked turkey
½ cup finely chopped unpeeled
  cucumber
½ cup mayonnaise or salad
  dressing

12 Basic Main Dish Crepes
  (see recipe, page 11)
1 teaspoon cornstarch
1 16-ounce can whole cranberry
  sauce

For filling: Combine turkey, cucumber, and mayonnaise *or* salad dressing.

To assemble: Spread 3 tablespoons filling onto unbrowned side of crepe, leaving ¼-inch rim around edge. Roll up crepe as for jelly roll. Place seam side down in a 13x9x2-inch baking dish. Repeat with remaining crepes. Cover with foil. Bake at 375° for 20 minutes.

For Cranberry Sauce: In small sauccpan stir cornstarch into whole cranberry sauce. Cook and stir till thickened and bubbly. Remove crepes from baking dish. Spoon sauce over each serving. Makes 6 servings.

Stuffed Chicken in a Crepe

6 *chicken thighs (1¼ pounds)*
2 *tablespoons butter*
1 *chicken bouillon cube*
3 *tablespoons all-purpose flour*
¼ *teaspoon paprika*
¾ *cup light cream*

1 *6-ounce can sliced mushrooms*
¼ *cup dry white wine*
3 *brown-and-serve sausage links,*
   halved lengthwise
6 *Basic Main Dish Crepes (see*
   recipe, page 11)

For sauce: Brown the chicken in butter. Dissolve bouillon cube in ½ cup boiling water; add to chicken. Cover; simmer till tender, 20 to 30 minutes. Remove chicken; cool slightly. Carefully remove bones; discard. Skim fat off broth; measure broth. Add enough water to make ¾ cup liquid. Return to skillet. Combine flour, paprika, ½ teaspoon salt, and dash pepper; blend in cream. Add to broth; cook and stir till sauce is thickened and bubbly. Drain mushrooms; stir mushrooms and wine into broth.

To assemble: Insert a sausage half in bone cavity of each thigh; place in center of unbrowned side of crepe. Top with 1 tablespoon sauce. Fold two opposite edges so they overlap atop chicken. Place seam side down in 12x-7½x2-inch baking dish. Repeat with remaining crepes. Spoon remaining sauce over. Cover; bake at 375° about 25 minutes. Makes 6 servings.

Chicken Curry Crepes

2 *slices bacon*
¼ *cup thinly sliced celery*
¼ *cup chopped onion*
1 *clove garlic, minced*
2 *tablespoons all-purpose flour*
1½ *cups milk*
½ *cup applesauce*
3 *tablespoons tomato paste*

1 *tablespoon curry powder*
2 *teaspoons instant chicken*
   bouillon granules
2 *cups cubed cooked chicken*
½ *cup chutney, cut up*
12 *Basic Main Dish Crepes (see*
   recipe, page 11)

For sauce: Cook bacon; drain and crumble. Reserve drippings. Cook celery, onion, and garlic in drippings. Blend in flour; add next 5 ingredients. Cook and stir till bubbly. Add chicken and bacon; heat through.

To assemble: Spread chutney over unbrowned side of crepe. Fold in half. Fold in half again, forming a triangle. Place in greased 13x9x2-inch baking dish. Repeat with remaining crepes. Cover; bake at 375° for 15 to 20 minutes. Spoon sauce over crepes. Top with toasted coconut or chopped peanuts, if desired. Makes 6 servings.

Mole-Sauced Chicken Crepes

Instant mashed potatoes
   (enough for 4 servings)
½ cup dairy sour cream
2 tablespoons chopped onion
2 tablespoons snipped parsley
14 to 16 Yellow Cornmeal Crepes
   (see recipe, page 13)
¼ cup chopped onion
¼ cup chopped green pepper
1 small clove garlic, minced
2 tablespoons butter
1 16-ounce can tomatoes, cut up

1 tablespoon sugar
2 teaspoons instant beef
   bouillon granules
1 teaspoon chili powder
¼ of a 1-ounce square
   unsweetened chocolate
¼ teaspoon ground cinnamon
¼ teaspoon ground nutmeg
   Dash ground cloves
   Dash bottled hot pepper sauce
3 cups chopped cooked chicken
2 tablespoons cornstarch

For filling: Prepare potatoes as directed on package, *except* omit ⅓ cup of the water. Blend in sour cream, 2 tablespoons onion, and parsley.

To assemble: Spoon 3 tablespoons filling in center of unbrowned side of crepe. Fold two opposite edges of crepe so they overlap atop filling. Fold in remaining edges, forming a square packet. Place seam side down in a greased 13x9x2-inch baking dish. Repeat with remaining crepes. Cover and bake at 375° till heated through, 25 to 30 minutes.

For sauce: Cook ¼ cup onion, green pepper, and garlic in butter till tender. Add next 9 ingredients, 1 cup water, and ½ teaspoon salt. Cook and stir till chocolate melts. Add chicken. Blend 2 tablespoons cold water into cornstarch; stir into sauce. Cook and stir till thickened and bubbly. Serve over hot crepes. Makes 7 or 8 servings.

Chicken with Artichokes

For sauce: Combine one 15½-ounce jar meatless spaghetti sauce and ½ cup dry sherry. Reserve ½ *cup* of the mixture; set aside. Stir one 9-ounce package frozen artichoke hearts, cooked and drained, and one 2½-ounce jar sliced mushrooms, drained, into the remaining mixture.

For filling: Mix 2 cups chopped cooked chicken and reserved ½ cup sauce.

To assemble: Using 12 Basic Main Dish Crepes (see recipe, page 11), spoon about 2 tablespoons filling along center of unbrowned side of crepe. Fold two opposite edges of crepe so they overlap atop filling. Place in a 13x9x2-inch baking dish. Repeat with remaining crepes. Cover; bake at 375° for 25 to 30 minutes. Heat the remaining sauce and spoon over individual servings. Makes 6 servings.

Fish and seafood

Shrimp Chow Mein Dinner

1½ pounds fresh or frozen
   shelled shrimp
¼ cup cooking oil
1 16-ounce can bean sprouts
1 medium onion, sliced
2 cups sliced fresh mushrooms
1 cup shredded cabbage or
   bok choy
1 6-ounce package frozen pea pods,
   thawed and halved crosswise

½ cup sliced water chestnuts
1 clove garlic, minced
1 13¾-ounce can chicken broth
¼ cup soy sauce
¼ teaspoon salt
3 tablespoons cornstarch
6 to 8 Oven-Baked Crepe Cups
   (see recipe, page 16)
½ cup toasted slivered almonds
   Soy sauce

For sauce: Thaw frozen shrimp; halve lengthwise, if desired. Cook and stir shrimp in hot oil for 1 to 2 minutes; remove. Drain sprouts; halve onion slices. Add sprouts, onion, mushrooms, cabbage, pea pods, water chestnuts, and garlic to oil. Cook and stir 2 to 3 minutes. Add *1¼ cups* of chicken broth, ¼ cup soy, and salt. Cover; simmer 6 to 8 minutes. Add shrimp to vegetables. Blend remaining broth into cornstarch; stir into mixture in skillet. Cook and stir till thickened and bubbly.

To assemble: Serve in baked crepe cups; garnish with almonds. Pass additional soy sauce. Makes 6 to 8 servings.

Avocado-Sauced Tuna Crepes

1 cup dairy sour cream
1 tablespoon snipped parsley
¼ teaspoon onion powder
1 9¼-ounce can tuna, drained
   and flaked
¼ cup finely chopped celery

8 Yellow Cornmeal Crepes (see
   recipe, page 13)
1 6-ounce carton frozen
   avocado dip, thawed
   Dash bottled hot pepper sauce

For filling: Combine ¾ cup of the sour cream, the snipped parsley, and onion powder. Fold in the tuna and chopped celery.

To assemble: Spread about 3 tablespoons tuna filling over unbrowned side of crepe, leaving ¼-inch rim around edge. Roll up crepe as for jelly roll. Place seam side down in 10x6x2-inch baking dish. Repeat with remaining crepes. Cover with foil. Bake at 350° for 20 to 25 minutes.

For sauce: Combine avocado dip, pepper sauce, and remaining ¼ cup sour cream. Spoon avocado sauce over hot crepes. Garnish with avocado slices and watercress, if desired. Makes 4 servings.

Choose crepes as a tasty new way to serve fish and seafood. In
Avocado-Sauced Tuna Crepes, a tangy mixture fills cornmeal crepes, while crepe cups hold *Shrimp Chow Mein Dinner.*

Calorie Counter's Fish Crepes

1 *16-ounce package frozen
    fish fillets, thawed*
1 *8-ounce can tomatoes, cut up*
1 *medium cucumber, peeled,
    seeded, and chopped (1 cup)*
1 *medium onion, finely chopped*
1 *tablespoon snipped parsley*

½ *teaspoon paprika*
¼ *teaspoon dried tarragon,
    crushed*
1 *tablespoon cold water*
2 *teaspoons cornstarch*
8 *Calorie Counter's Crepes (see
    recipe, page 11)*

For filling: Place fish in greased skillet. Add boiling water to cover and 1 teaspoon salt. Simmer, covered, till fish flakes easily with fork, about 5 minutes. Carefully remove fish; flake, removing skin and bones. In sauce-pan combine tomatoes, cucumber, onion, parsley, paprika, tarragon, ½ teaspoon salt, and ⅛ teaspoon pepper. Simmer, covered, for 20 minutes. Slowly blend cold water into cornstarch; stir into tomato mixture. Cook and stir till thickened and bubbly. Set aside *1 cup* of the mixture. Stir remaining mixture into fish.

To assemble: Spoon about 3 tablespoons fish mixture down center of un-browned side of each crepe; roll up. Place seam side down in 12x7½x2-inch baking dish. Bake, covered, at 375° till heated through, about 20 minutes. Reheat reserved tomato mixture; spoon over crepes. Serves 4.

Scallop Crepe Dinner

1½ *pounds frozen scallops*
1 *9-ounce package frozen
    Italian green beans
    Mornay Sauce with Wine
    (see recipe, page 17)*

12 *Basic Main Dish Crepes (see
    recipe, page 11)*
2 *tablespoons light cream*
1 *tablespoon toasted slivered
    almonds*

For filling: Thaw scallops. Bring 4 cups water and 2 teaspoons salt to boiling. Add scallops; return to boiling. Reduce heat; simmer, covered, 2 minutes. Drain and halve scallops. Cook beans according to package directions; drain. Prepare sauce, *except* use 1½ cups light cream instead of the 1 cup light cream called for. Stir in scallops and beans.

To assemble: Spoon about ¼ cup of the filling down center of unbrowned side of crepe; roll up. Place seam side down in 13x9x2-inch baking dish. Repeat with remaining crepes. Stir 2 tablespoons light cream into remaining filling; spoon over crepes. Cover; bake at 375° about 25 minutes. Sprinkle with almonds. Makes 6 servings.

Crab and Shrimp Torte

For crepes: Using Feathery Sour Cream Crepes batter (see recipe, page 14) prepare 24 crepes by spooning 1 tablespoon batter for each crepe into a hot lightly greased 6-inch skillet and spreading with back of spoon into a 4-inch circle. Brown on one side only.

For sauce: In saucepan cook 1 cup sliced fresh mushrooms and ¼ cup finely chopped onion in ¼ cup butter. Blend in ⅓ cup all-purpose flour, and ¼ teaspoon salt. Add 1½ cups milk. Cook and stir till thickened and bubbly. Stir in one 7½-ounce can crab meat, drained, flaked, and cartilage removed; one 4½-ounce can shrimp; and 3 tablespoons dry sherry.

To assemble: Place six crepes, browned side down and equal distance apart, on a greased baking sheet. Spread about 3 tablespoons crab sauce over each crepe. Repeat layering crepes *(browned side up)* and sauce two more times. Top with another crepe, making six stacks of 4 crepes each. Bake crepe stacks at 350° till heated through, 20 to 25 minutes. Sprinkle crepes with ¾ cup shredded gruyere cheese; return to oven till cheese melts. Sprinkle with paprika. Makes 6 servings.

Double Cheese Fish Crepes

1 *16-ounce package frozen fish fillets, thawed*
¼ *cup finely chopped onion*
¼ *cup finely chopped celery*
2 *tablespoons butter*
2 *tablespoons all-purpose flour*
¼ *teaspoon dried dillweed*
1¼ *cups milk*
½ *cup shredded sharp American cheese (2 ounces)*
½ *cup shredded process Swiss cheese (2 ounces)*
10 *Whole Wheat Crepes (see recipe, page 14)*

For filling: Place fish in greased skillet. Add boiling water to cover and 1 teaspoon salt. Simmer, covered, till fish flakes easily with fork, about 5 minutes. Carefully remove fish; flake, removing any skin and bones. In saucepan cook onion and celery in butter till tender; blend in flour, dillweed, and ¼ teaspoon salt. Add milk. Cook and stir till thickened and bubbly. Remove from heat; stir in cheeses till melted. Set aside *1 cup* of the mixture. Stir fish into remaining mixture.

To assemble: Spoon about 3 tablespoons of the fish mixture down center of unbrowned side of crepe; roll up. Place seam side down in 12x7½x2-inch baking dish. Repeat with remaining crepes. Pour the reserved 1 cup cheese mixture over the crepes. Cover and bake at 375° till heated through, 20 to 25 minutes. Makes 5 servings.

High-Top Shrimp Crepes

A fluffy baked egg sauce tops this fancy seafood crepe shown on pages 20-21—

1 *10-ounce package frozen
  asparagus spears*
1 *4½-ounce can medium shrimp* or
  *one 6½- or 7-ounce can tuna,
  drained and flaked*
⅓ *cup mayonnaise* or *salad
  dressing*
¼ *cup finely chopped celery*
1 *tablespoon finely chopped
  pimiento*

3 *egg yolks*
¼ *teaspoon salt*
  Dash pepper
¼ *cup mayonnaise* or *salad
  dressing*
3 *egg whites*
6 *Whole Wheat Crepes
  (see recipe, page 14)*
¾ *cup shredded Swiss cheese
  (3 ounces)*

For filling: In saucepan cook asparagus according to package directions; drain well. Set aside 6 shrimp. In small bowl combine remaining shrimp, ⅓ cup mayonnaise, celery, and pimiento.

For sauce: In mixing bowl beat egg yolks, salt, and pepper till thick and lemon-colored; stir in the ¼ cup mayonnaise. In mixing bowl beat egg whites with electric mixer till stiff peaks form. Carefully fold egg yolk mixture into beaten egg whites.

To assemble: Place the crepes, browned side up and equal distance apart, on greased baking sheet. Spread each crepe with about 3 tablespoons shrimp filling. Sprinkle with Swiss cheese. Place asparagus spears atop. Spoon egg mixture over the asparagus. Bake at 350° till topping is golden brown and filling is warm, about 15 minutes. Use wide spatula to transfer crepes to individual serving plates. Garnish with reserved shrimp. Serve immediately. Makes 6 crepes.

*Cooking Tips
for Crepes*

Before cooking in your crepe pan or skillet for the first time, season the inside by rubbing generously with cooking oil. Then, heat over medium heat for 5 minutes; remove. Allow the pan to cool. If possible, let stand overnight.

Use the water-drop test to determine when the crepe pan is the right cooking temperature. As the pan is preheating over medium heat, sprinkle a few drops of water in the pan. If the drops sizzle and bounce, the pan is the right cooking temperature.

When cooking crepes, brown them on one side only. When done, the tops will look dry and the edges will curl; this takes about 45 to 60 seconds each.

Blue Cheese-Sauced Fish Crepes

1 12-ounce package frozen
   halibut steaks, thawed
1 cup dairy sour cream
1 tablespoon all-purpose flour
½ cup milk

¼ cup crumbled blue cheese
   Dash bottled hot pepper sauce
8 Basic Main Dish Crepes (see
   recipe, page 11)
1 sliced green onion with top

For filling: Place fish in greased skillet. Add boiling water to cover and 1 teaspoon salt. Simmer, covered, till fish flakes easily with fork, about 5 minutes. Carefully remove fish; flake, removing skin and bones. In saucepan combine sour cream and flour. Add milk, blue cheese, pepper sauce, and ¼ teaspoon salt. Cook and stir till thickened (do not boil). Set aside *1 cup* mixture. Stir remainder into fish.

To assemble: Spoon about 2 tablespoons fish mixture down center of unbrowned side of each crepe; roll up. Place seam side down in 12x7½x2-inch baking dish. Cover; bake at 375° about 20 minutes. Reheat reserved mixture; spoon over crepes. Garnish with green onion. Makes 4 servings.

Quiche in a Crepe

Basic Main Dish Crepes batter
   (see recipe, page 11)
3 beaten eggs
1 cup light cream
¼ teaspoon grated lemon peel
¼ teaspoon dry mustard
   Dash ground mace

1 cup shredded monterey jack
   cheese
1 6½- or 7-ounce can tuna,
   drained and flaked
½ cup finely chopped celery
¼ cup finely chopped onion
¼ cup sliced almonds

For crepes: Using ¼ cup batter for each, prepare 8 crepes by spooning batter into a hot lightly greased 10-inch skillet. Lift and tilt pan to spread batter. Brown one side of crepe only.

For filling: Mix eggs, cream, peel, mustard, mace, and ½ teaspoon salt.

To assemble: Place *two* crepes unbrowned sides together in *each* of four greased 10-ounce casseroles. Carefully arrange ruffled tops. Sprinkle ¼ *cup* cheese in bottom of *each* crepe cup. Divide tuna, celery, and onion among cups. Spoon about ½ *cup* egg mixture into *each* cup. Sprinkle with almonds. Set in shallow baking pan on oven rack. Pour hot water around casseroles in pan to depth of 1 inch. Bake, uncovered, at 350° till knife inserted off-center comes out clean, about 35 minutes. Remove from oven; let stand 10 minutes. Makes 4 servings.

Pork and ham

Brunch Crepes with Apple Rings

Serve this attractive main dish, shown on pages 20-21, as a hearty supper dish, too—

4 *medium cooking apples, cored*
½ *cup honey*
2 *tablespoons vinegar*
¼ *teaspoon ground cinnamon*
10 *fresh pork sausage links*
¼ *cup water*

¼ *cup chopped onion*
1 *tablespoon all-purpose flour*
1 *cup apple cider* or *apple juice*
10 *Basic Main Dish Crepes (see recipe, page 11)*
2 *teaspoons finely snipped parsley*

For apple rings: Cut unpeeled apples in ½-inch rings. In skillet bring honey, vinegar, cinnamon, and ¼ teaspoon salt just to boiling. Add apples; cook, turning often, till transparent, 10 to 12 minutes. Drain.

For sauce: Prick sausage links with fork. In skillet cook links in water, covered, for 5 minutes. Drain. Cook, uncovered, till links are browned. Pour off drippings, reserving 2 tablespoons. Set links aside. Cook onion in reserved drippings till tender. Blend in flour and ¼ teaspoon salt; add cider. Cook and stir till thickened and bubbly.

To assemble: Spoon small amount of sauce in center of unbrowned side of crepe. Fold crepe in half. Fold in half again to form a triangle. Place in chafing dish or skillet. Repeat with remaining crepes. Arrange sausage and apple rings with crepes. Spoon remaining sauce over all. Cover; heat through. Sprinkle with parsley before serving. Serves 5.

Layered Crepes Florentine

1 *pound bulk Italian sausage* or *bulk pork sausage*
1 *15½-ounce jar spaghetti sauce with mushrooms*
12 *Basic Main Dish Crepes (see recipe, page 11)*

1 *cup cream-style cottage cheese*
1 *10-ounce package frozen chopped spinach, cooked and well drained*
2 *tablespoons grated parmesan cheese*

For sauce: In a skillet slowly brown sausage; pour off excess fat. Add spaghetti sauce. Simmer, uncovered, for 10 minutes.

To assemble: Arrange 6 crepes in a single layer in greased 12x7½x2-inch baking dish, overlapping edges so that bottom of dish is well covered. Layer crepes with *half* of the cottage cheese and *half* of the sauce. Place spinach atop. Repeat layering with remaining crepes, cottage cheese, and sauce. Sprinkle with parmesan. Cover; bake at 375° about 20 minutes. Let stand 5 minutes before serving. Makes 4 to 6 servings.

When preparing *Ham and Apricot Crepes* for company, make the crepes ahead. At serving time, roll up crepes with ham inside and heat in the fruit sauce.
For an impressive finale, pour flaming brandy over the crepes and apricots.

Ham and Apricot Crepes

For sauce: Drain one 8¾-ounce can unpeeled apricot halves; reserve syrup. Set apricots aside. In saucepan mix ⅔ cup sugar, 2 tablespoons cornstarch, and dash salt. Blend in reserved syrup. Add one 12-ounce can apricot nectar. Cook and stir till bubbly. Remove from heat; add 2 teaspoons lemon juice. Stir in 2 tablespoons butter till melted.
To assemble: Using 10 slices boiled ham and 10 Basic Main Dish Crepes (see recipe, page 11), place a ham slice on unbrowned side of crepe; roll up as for jelly roll. Place seam side down in chafing dish or skillet. Repeat with remaining crepes. Add apricots; pour sauce over all. Cover and heat through. If desired, heat ¼ cup brandy in a ladle or small pan. Remove cover from chafing dish. Flame brandy and pour over crepes; stir brandy into sauce when flame dies down. Serves 5.

Home-Style Pork Pie Crepes

1 *pound ground pork*
½ *cup finely chopped onion*
¼ *cup fine dry bread crumbs*
1 *teaspoon salt*
⅛ *teaspoon ground sage*
12 *Tangy Buttermilk Crepes (see recipe, page 11)*

2 *tablespoons butter* or *margarine*
2 *tablespoons all-purpose flour*
2 *cups milk*
• • •
¼ *cup snipped parsley*
Ground nutmeg

For filling: In skillet brown pork; drain off fat. Stir in onion, bread crumbs, salt, sage, ¾ cup water, and dash pepper. Simmer, covered, till pork is done and onion is tender, about 20 minutes.

To assemble: Spread about ¼ cup filling over unbrowned side of crepe, leaving ¼-inch rim around edge. Roll up crepe as for jelly roll. Place seam side down in 13x9x2-inch baking dish. Repeat with remaining crepes. Bake, covered, at 375° about 20 minutes.

For sauce: Melt butter; blend in flour, 1 teaspoon salt, and dash pepper. Add milk. Cook and stir till bubbly. Cook 2 to 3 minutes more. Spoon sauce over crepes. Sprinkle with parsley and nutmeg. Serves 6.

Garden Salad Ham Crepes

2 *cups sliced cauliflowerets (½ medium head)*
2 *tablespoons chopped onion*
2 *tablespoons cooking oil*
2 *tablespoons cornstarch*
1 *tablespoon sugar*
1 *teaspoon prepared mustard*
½ *teaspoon garlic salt*

Dash pepper
⅓ *cup vinegar*
2 *cups diced fully cooked ham*
3 *cups shredded lettuce*
12 *Basic Main Dish Crepes (see recipe, page 11)*
Grated parmesan cheese
1 *cup halved cherry tomatoes*

For sauce: Cook cauliflower in boiling salted water till crisp-tender, 6 to 7 minutes. Drain; set aside. In 2-quart saucepan cook onion in hot oil till tender. Blend in cornstarch, sugar, mustard, garlic salt, and pepper. Stir in vinegar and ¾ cup water. Cook and stir till thickened and bubbly. Add ham and cauliflower; heat through.

To assemble: Place about ¼ cup lettuce along center of unbrowned side of crepe. Roll up crepe. Place seam side down on serving platter. Repeat with remaining crepes. Spoon sauce over crepes. Sprinkle with parmesan; garnish with tomatoes. Makes 6 servings.

Szekely-Filled Crepes

1 *medium potato*	1 *tablespoon butter* or *margarine*
⅓ *cup all-purpose flour*	1 *tablespoon all-purpose flour*
1 *cup milk*	1 *teaspoon paprika*
1 *egg*	½ *teaspoon caraway seed*
2 *teaspoons butter, softened*	1 *cup dairy sour cream*
⅛ *teaspoon baking powder*	1 *8-ounce can sauerkraut*
2 *tablespoons chopped onion*	2 *cups chopped cooked pork*

For Potato Crepes: Peel and quarter potato. Cook, covered, in boiling salted water till tender, 20 to 25 minutes. Drain. In blender container place potato, ⅓ cup flour, ½ *cup* milk, egg, 2 teaspoons butter, baking powder, ¼ teaspoon salt, and dash pepper. *(Or,* use ½ cup leftover mashed potatoes instead of cooked potato and omit the salt.) Cover; blend till smooth. Heat a lightly greased 6-inch skillet. Remove from heat; spoon in about 2 tablespoons batter. Lift and tilt skillet to spread batter evenly. Return to heat; brown on one side only, 45 to 60 seconds. *(Or* cook on inverted crepe pan, see page 8.) To remove, invert skillet or pan over paper toweling. Remove crepe. Repeat with remaining batter to make 12 crepes, greasing skillet occasionally.

For filling: Cook onion in 1 tablespoon butter till tender. Blend in 1 tablespoon flour, paprika, caraway, and ½ teaspoon salt. Add the remaining milk. Cook and stir till bubbly. Remove from heat. Blend in ½ *cup* sour cream. Drain sauerkraut; snip. Fold into milk mixture with pork.

To assemble: Spoon about ¼ cup filling along center of unbrowned side of crepe. Fold two opposite edges so they overlap atop filling. Place seam side down in 13x9x2-inch baking dish. Repeat with remaining crepes. Cover; bake at 375° for 25 to 30 minutes. Spoon remaining sour cream atop individual servings. Top with paprika, if desired. Makes 6 servings.

Asparagus-Ham Roll-Ups

For filling: Cook 16 to 24 fresh asparagus spears in small amount of boiling salted water till tender, 10 to 15 minutes. Drain well.

To assemble: Using 16 slices boiled ham and 8 Basic Main Dish Crepes (see recipe, page 11), place two ham slices on unbrowned side of each crepe. Place 2 or 3 asparagus spears in center of each crepe. Roll up crepe. Place seam side down in 12x7½x2-inch baking dish. Cover; bake at 350° till hot, about 20 minutes. Remove crepes from dish. Spoon Blender Hollandaise Sauce (see recipe, page 17) over crepes. Serves 4.

Beef

Sweet-Sour Burger Crepes

1 *13¼-ounce can pineapple*
  tidbits
⅓ *cup packed brown sugar*
2 *tablespoons cornstarch*
¼ *teaspoon salt*
⅛ *teaspoon ground ginger*
⅓ *cup vinegar*
1 *tablespoon soy sauce*

1 *medium green pepper, cut in*
  ½-inch cubes
¾ *pound ground beef*
½ *cup chopped onion*
12 *Basic Main Dish Crepes (see*
  recipe, page 11)
½ *teaspoon salt*
⅛ *teaspoon pepper*

For sauce: Drain pineapple, reserving syrup. Add enough water to syrup to make 1 cup. In saucepan combine brown sugar, cornstarch, ¼ teaspoon salt, and ginger. Blend in reserved syrup mixture. Add vinegar and soy sauce. Cook and stir till thickened and bubbly. Reserve ⅓ *cup* of the sauce. Stir pineapple and green pepper into the remaining sauce.

For filling: In medium skillet cook ground beef and onion till beef is browned and onion is tender. Drain off excess fat. Add the reserved ⅓ cup sauce, ½ teaspoon salt, and pepper.

To assemble: Spoon about 3 tablespoons filling along center of unbrowned side of each crepe. Fold opposite edges of each crepe so they overlap atop filling. Place seam side down in 13x9x2-inch baking dish. Cover; bake at 375° about 20 minutes. Reheat sauce; spoon over. Serves 6.

Beef Stroganoff Crepes

For filling: Cut 1 pound beef sirloin into 2x¼-inch strips; coat with mixture of 1 tablespoon all-purpose flour and ½ teaspoon salt. In skillet quickly brown beef on both sides in 2 tablespoons butter. Add one 2½-ounce jar sliced mushrooms, drained; ½ cup chopped onion; and 1 clove garlic, minced. Cook onion till crisp-tender, 3 to 4 minutes. Remove mixture from pan. Melt 2 tablespoons butter in pan; blend in 2 tablespoons all-purpose flour and 1 tablespoon tomato paste. Add ¾ cup beef broth. Cook and stir till thickened and bubbly. Stir in ½ cup dairy sour cream and 2 tablespoons dry white wine. Return meat mixture to pan.

To assemble: Using 12 Basic Main Dish Crepes (see recipe, page 11), spoon about 3 tablespoons filling along center of unbrowned side of crepe. Fold two opposite edges so they overlap atop filling. Place seam side down in 13x9x2-inch baking dish. Repeat with remaining crepes. Cover; bake at 375° till heated through, 15 to 20 minutes. Garnish individual servings with additional sour cream, if desired. Serves 6.

Greek-Style Crepe Casserole

1½ pounds ground beef
1 cup chopped onion
1 16-ounce can tomatoes, cut up
1 6-ounce can tomato paste
¼ teaspoon dried thyme, crushed
4 slightly beaten egg whites
½ cup cubed feta cheese or
   American cheese

½ cup butter or margarine
½ cup all-purpose flour
1 teaspoon salt
¼ teaspoon ground cinnamon
4 cups milk
4 slightly beaten egg yolks
16 Basic Main Dish Crepes (see
   recipe, page 11)

For filling: In skillet cook ground beef with onion. Drain off fat. Add undrained tomatoes, tomato paste, thyme, and 1 teaspoon salt. Simmer, covered, for 25 to 30 minutes, stirring often. Stir about half of the hot mixture into egg whites. Return to skillet; cook till thickened, 1 to 2 minutes longer. Remove from heat; stir in cheese.

For sauce: In saucepan melt butter; blend in flour, salt, and cinnamon. Add milk all at once. Cook and stir till thickened and bubbly. Remove from heat. Gradually blend about half of the hot mixture into egg yolks; return to remaining hot mixture, stirring rapidly. Remove from heat.

To assemble: Spread *half* of the filling in an ungreased 13x9x2-inch baking dish. Arrange 8 of the crepes atop, overlapping to fit dish. Repeat layers with remaining filling and crepes. Pour sauce over crepes. Sprinkle lightly with additional cinnamon, if desired. Bake, uncovered, at 375° till heated through and top is set, about 25 minutes. Let stand 10 minutes before serving. Makes 10 to 12 servings.

Crepe Problems

While experience will solve most crepe making difficulties, here are some solutions to common problems:

1) Batter sticks to pan. *Cause:* a) Pan is not properly oiled or seasoned. b) Heat is too low. *To solve:* a) Follow manufacturer's directions for oiling and seasoning pan. b) Increase the heat.

2) Batter runs off inverted crepe pan. *Cause:* Pan not hot enough. *To solve:* Increase the heat.

3) Batter won't swirl when spread in skillet. *Cause:* Batter is too thick. *To solve:* Gradually blend small amounts of milk or water into batter.

4) Crepes have dark, lacy "veins" throughout. *Cause:* a) Pan is either not hot enough or too hot. b) Pan is oiled too heavily. *To solve:* a) Adjust the heat to proper level. b) Wipe off excess oil.

If your family enjoys highly seasoned foods, they'll love this version of a
Mexican enchilada, *Beef Enchilada Crepes*. This main dish gets its
peppy flavor from the jalapeño bean dip, chili powder, and hot pepper sauce.

Beef Enchilada Crepes

For filling: Cook 1 pound ground beef with ½ cup chopped onion and ½
cup chopped green pepper (optional). Drain off fat. Blend in one 10½-
ounce can jalapeño bean dip, ½ teaspoon salt, and ⅛ teaspoon pepper.
For sauce: Mix 3 tablespoons all-purpose flour, ½ teaspoon salt, ¼ teaspoon chili powder, and ¼ teaspoon paprika. Add 1½ cups milk and several dashes bottled hot pepper sauce. Cook and stir till bubbly. Stir in ¾
cup shredded sharp American cheese and ¼ cup pitted ripe olives, sliced.
To assemble: Using 12 Yellow Cornmeal Crepes (see recipe, page 13),
spread about ¼ cup filling over unbrowned side of crepe, leaving ¼-inch
rim around edge. Roll up as for jelly roll. Place seam side down in 13x9x2-
inch baking dish. Repeat with remaining crepes. Pour sauce over. Cover;
bake at 375° till heated through, 25 to 30 minutes. Serves 6.

Individual Beef Wellingtons

Feathery Sour Cream Crepes
butter (see recipe, page 14)
8 4- to 5-ounce pieces of beef
tenderloin
2 tablespoons cooking oil

2 2¾-ounce cans liver paté
Golden Béchamel Sauce (see
recipe, page 17)
Snipped parsley

For crepes: Using ¼ cup batter for each, prepare eight 8- *or* 10-inch crepes by spooning batter into a hot lightly greased 8- *or* 10-inch skillet. Lift and tilt pan to spread batter. Brown on one side only.

To assemble: Brown fillets in hot oil for 5 minutes per side. Drain; wrap. Chill. Before serving, spread one side of meat with paté. Center a fillet, paté-side down, on unbrowned side of each crepe. Draw crepe sides up around meat; secure with wooden picks, if needed. Place seam side down in greased shallow baking pan. Bake, uncovered, at 450° 10 minutes for rare; 12 minutes for medium-rare; and 15 minutes for medium. Remove picks. Serve with sauce; top with parsley. Serves 8.

Crepe-Style Manicotti

½ pound ground beef
½ cup chopped onion
1 small clove garlic, minced
1 8-ounce can tomatoes, cut up
1 6-ounce can tomato paste
1½ teaspoons dried basil,
    crushed
½ teaspoon sugar
¼ teaspoon fennel seed, crushed
2 beaten eggs

3 cups ricotta or cream-
    style cottage cheese
¼ cup grated parmesan cheese
1 tablespoon dried parsley
    flakes
½ teaspoon salt
¼ teaspoon pepper
16 Basic Main Dish Crepes (see
    recipe, page 11)
1 cup shredded mozzarella cheese

For sauce: Brown ground beef with onion and garlic. Drain. Add undrained tomatoes, tomato paste, basil, sugar, fennel, ½ cup water, and ¾ teaspoon salt. Simmer, covered, about 15 minutes, stirring often.

For filling: Mix eggs, ricotta, parmesan, parsley, salt, and pepper.

To assemble: Spoon about 3 tablespoons filling along center of unbrowned side of crepe. Fold two opposite edges so they overlap atop filling. Place seam side down in 13x9x2-inch baking dish. Repeat with remaining crepes. Spoon sauce over. Cover; bake at 375° for 25 minutes. Uncover; sprinkle with mozzarella. Bake till cheese melts. Makes 8 servings.

Crepe assortment

Coney Island Crepes

¼ cup chopped onion
¼ cup chopped green pepper
¼ cup water
1 15-ounce can chili with beans
 Dash bottled hot pepper sauce
½ cup tomato sauce

6 frankfurters, cut in half
 lengthwise
12 Tangy Buttermilk Crepes (see
 recipe, page 11)
½ cup shredded American cheese
 (2 ounces)

For sauce: In saucepan cook onion and green pepper in water, covered, for 2 minutes. *Do not drain.* Stir in chili and pepper sauce. Set aside ⅔ cup chili mixture. Stir tomato sauce into remaining mixture.

To assemble: Place one frankfurter half on unbrowned side of each crepe. Top with about 1 tablespoon reserved chili mixture; roll up. Place crepes seam side down in 13x9x2-inch baking dish. Cover; bake at 375° till meat is hot, 20 to 25 minutes. Heat remaining tomato sauce mixture; pour over crepes. Sprinkle with cheese. Makes 6 servings.

Sweet-Sour Frankfurter Crepes

1 8¼-ounce can pineapple slices
1 medium onion, chopped (½ cup)
1 medium green pepper, chopped
2 tablespoons butter or
 margarine
2 tablespoons cornstarch
2 tablespoons brown sugar
1 teaspoon instant beef
 bouillon granules

Dash salt
1 cup water
2 tablespoons vinegar
1 tablespoon soy sauce
6 frankfurters, cut crosswise
 in ¼-inch slices
12 Basic Main Dish Crepes
 (see recipe, page 11)

For filling: Drain pineapple, reserving syrup. Cut pineapple into small pieces; set aside. In skillet cook onion and green pepper in butter till vegetables are tender but not brown. Combine cornstarch, brown sugar, bouillon granules, and salt. Stir into onion mixture. Blend in reserved pineapple syrup, water, vinegar, and soy sauce. Cook and stir till mixture is thickened and bubbly. Add franks and pineapple.

To assemble: Spoon about 3 tablespoons filling along center of unbrowned side of each crepe. Fold two opposite edges of crepe so they overlap atop filling. Place *seam side up* in 13x9x2-inch baking dish. Spoon remaining filling over crepes. Cover; bake at 375° till heated through, 20 to 25 minutes. Makes 6 servings.

Liver and Tomatoes in Crepes

6 slices bacon
¾ cup chopped onion
1 clove garlic, minced
2 tablespoons all-purpose
    flour
¾ teaspoon salt
¾ teaspoon chili powder
    Dash pepper

½ pound beef liver, cut cross-
    wise in ¼-inch strips
1 16-ounce can tomatoes, cut up
1 8¾-ounce can whole kernel corn
2 tablespoons cornstarch
¼ teaspoon salt
12 Yellow Cornmeal Crepes
    (see recipe, page 13)

For filling: In large skillet cook bacon till crisp. Drain, reserving 3 table-spoons drippings in skillet. Crumble bacon and set aside. Cook onion and garlic in drippings till onion is tender. Combine flour, the ¾ teaspoon salt, chili powder, and pepper. Add liver; toss till coated. Add liver to onion in skillet; brown quickly on all sides.

For sauce: In medium saucepan blend undrained tomatoes and undrained corn into cornstarch; add the ¼ teaspoon salt. Cook and stir till mixture is thickened and bubbly. Stir in crumbled bacon.

To assemble: Spoon liver filling along center of unbrowned side of crepes, dividing mixture among crepes. Place 1 tablespoon tomato sauce atop each crepe. Fold two opposite edges of each crepe so they overlap atop filling. Place crepes seam side down in 13x9x2-inch baking dish. Spoon remaining sauce over crepes. Cover; bake at 375° till heated through, 20 to 25 minutes. Makes 6 servings.

Chicken Liver Crepe Cups

6 slices bacon
1 pound chicken livers, cut up
1 10¾-ounce can condensed
    cream of chicken soup
⅓ cup milk

1 3-ounce package cream cheese,
    softened
6 Oven-Baked Crepe Cups (see
    recipe, page 16)
2 tablespoons snipped parsley

For sauce: In skillet cook bacon till crisp. Drain, reserving 2 tablespoons drippings. Crumble bacon; set aside. Cook half the livers at a time in drippings just till slightly pink in center, about 5 minutes. Remove from skillet. Repeat with second half. In same skillet heat soup till bubbly. Blend milk into cream cheese; stir into soup. Add dash pepper. Cook and stir till bubbly. Add livers and bacon; heat through.

To assemble: Spoon sauce into crepe cups. Top with parsley. Serves 6.

Lamb with Tarragon Sauce

1 pound lamb stew meat, cut in
   ½-inch cubes
1 cup chopped onion
1 cup chopped carrot
½ cup chopped celery
2 tablespoons snipped parsley
1 teaspoon dried oregano,
   crushed
1 teaspoon dried tarragon,
   crushed

1 bay leaf
10 Basic Main Dish Crepes
   (see recipe, page 11)
1 tablespoon butter
1 tablespoon all-purpose flour
1 teaspoon sugar
¼ teaspoon dried tarragon,
   crushed
2 tablespoons dry sherry
1 beaten egg yolk

For filling: Combine lamb, onion, carrot, celery, parsley, oregano, 1 teaspoon tarragon, bay leaf, and 1½ teaspoons salt; add 3 cups water. Cover; simmer till meat is tender, about 50 minutes. Season. Strain meat and vegetables, reserving ¾ cup cooking liquid; set aside.

To assemble: Spoon about 3 tablespoons lamb filling down center of unbrowned side of each crepe. Fold two opposite edges of each crepe so they overlap atop filling. Place crepes seam side down in 12x7½x2-inch baking dish. Cover; bake at 375° till hot, about 25 minutes.

For Tarragon Sauce: In small saucepan melt butter; blend in flour, sugar, and the ¼ teaspoon tarragon. Stir in the ¾ cup reserved cooking liquid and sherry. Cook, stirring constantly, till thickened and bubbly. Gradually stir about half of the hot mixture into beaten egg yolk; return to hot mixture. Cook, stirring constantly, 1 to 2 minutes more. To serve, pour hot sauce over the crepes. Makes 5 servings.

Dill-Sauced Lamb Rolls

For filling: Combine 1 beaten egg, 1 cup finely chopped peeled eggplant, ¼ cup soft bread crumbs, ¼ cup finely chopped onion, ¾ teaspoon salt, and dash pepper. Add 1 pound ground lamb; mix well. Shape mixture into 10 logs, about 4 inches long. In skillet brown logs on all sides in 2 tablespoons cooking oil, about 12 minutes. Drain well.

For sauce: Prepare Creamy Velouté Sauce (see recipe, page 17). Stir in ½ teaspoon dried dillweed.

To assemble: Using 10 Basic Main Dish Crepes (see recipe, page 11), place one meat log on unbrowned side of each crepe; roll up. Place seam side down in a 12x7½x2-inch baking dish. Spoon sauce over. Cover; bake at 375° till heated through, about 20 minutes. Makes 5 servings.

Participation crepes

Let cooking be part of the evening's fun at your next dinner party. Here's how. Either fix the crepes, sauce, and an array of fillings ahead and let your guests assemble their own combinations or make the filling and sauces and let your guests try baking their own crepes either in a skillet or in an inverted crepe pan.

Pizza Dinner Bundles

2 recipes Basic Main Dish Crepes
   batter (see recipe, page 11)
Bulk pizza sausage or ground
   beef, cooked and drained
Diced fully cooked ham
Chopped Canadian-style bacon
Sliced pepperoni
Sliced salami, cut in strips
Canned shrimp, drained

Canned anchovies, drained
Sliced fresh mushrooms
Finely chopped onion
Finely chopped green pepper
Sliced olives
Shredded mozzarella, cheddar,
   or monterey jack cheese
Grated parmesan cheese
Pizza Sauce for Bundles

For crepes: Using ¼ cup batter for each, prepare 18 crepes by spooning batter into a hot lightly greased 10-inch skillet. Lift and tilt skillet to spread batter evenly. Return to heat; brown on one side only. To remove crepe, invert pan over paper toweling.

To assemble: Choose as many fillings as you need for the number of guests. Plan to use about ⅓ cup meat and vegetables for each bundle. Place filling in center of unbrowned side of crepe; top with 2 tablespoons desired cheese. Overlap 2 opposite edges of crepe atop filling; fold in remaining edges forming a square packet. Place seam side down on greased baking sheet. Bake at 375° till hot, 18 to 20 minutes. Serve with pizza sauce and more cheese. Makes 18.

Pizza Sauce for Bundles

In saucepan cook 1 cup chopped onion and 1 clove garlic, minced, in 2 tablespoons cooking oil till tender. Add one 16-ounce can tomatoes, cut up; one 6-ounce can tomato paste; 2 tablespoons dried parsley flakes; 1½ teaspoons dried basil, crushed; 1½ teaspoons dried oregano, crushed; 1 teaspoon salt; ½ teaspoon sugar; and ⅛ teaspoon pepper. Bring to boiling. Cover; and simmer 10 minutes, stirring once or twice. Transfer sauce to fondue pot; place over burner. Makes about 3 cups.

Chinese-Style Dinner

½ pound finely chopped
   boneless pork
1 clove garlic, minced
1 tablespoon cooking oil
2 cups finely shredded bok choy
   or cabbage
1 cup chopped fresh mushrooms
½ cup each finely chopped onion,
   celery, and water chestnuts
¼ cup shredded carrot

1 4½-ounce can shrimp, drained
   and chopped
1 beaten egg
2 tablespoons soy sauce
1 tablespoon dry sherry
½ teaspoon sugar
32 Basic Main Dish Crepes (see
   recipe, page 11)
Sweet and Sour Sauce
Horseradish-Mustard Sauce

For filling: In skillet cook pork and garlic quickly in hot oil, stirring till meat is browned. Drain off fat. Add vegetables; cook and stir 2 to 3 minutes more. In bowl combine pork-vegetable mixture with shrimp, egg, soy, sherry, sugar, and ¼ teaspoon salt. Cool.

To assemble: Spoon about 2 tablespoons filling near edge of unbrowned side of crepe. Fold edge nearest filling up and over filling just till mixture is covered, fold in the two sides, then roll up tightly as for jelly roll. Place seam side down in greased 15½x10½x1-inch baking pan. Repeat with remaining crepes. Bake, uncovered, at 375° for 18 to 20 minutes. Serve with sauces. Makes 32 roll-ups.

Sweet and Sour Sauce

In saucepan combine ½ cup packed brown sugar and 1 tablespoon cornstarch. Stir in ⅓ cup red wine vinegar, ⅓ cup chicken broth, ¼ cup finely chopped green pepper, 2 tablespoons chopped pimiento, 1 tablespoon soy sauce, ¼ teaspoon garlic powder, and ¼ teaspoon ground ginger. Cook and stir till bubbly. Serve hot. Makes 1¼ cups sauce.

Horseradish-Mustard Sauce

Melt 1 tablespoon butter; blend in 2 tablespoons Dijon-style mustard, 1 tablespoon all-purpose flour, 1 tablespoon prepared horseradish, ¼ teaspoon salt, several drops bottled hot pepper sauce, and dash white pepper. Add ½ cup chicken broth and ½ cup milk *or* light cream. Cook and stir till bubbly. Remove from heat; stir in 2 teaspoons snipped chives and 1 teaspoon lemon juice. Serve hot. Makes 1¼ cups.

Give a participation *Chinese-Style Dinner*. Have your guests
prepare, fill, and bake their own crepes. Then, serve the
bundles with *Sweet and Sour Sauce* and *Horseradish-Mustard Sauce*.

Crepes around the world

Although the crepe is of French origin, cultures the world over use thin pancakes in cooking. Here, you'll find main dishes from Sweden, Russia, and China; and on page 87 Jewish and Italian desserts.

Swedish Pancake Roll-Ups

For crepes: In bowl combine ½ cup all-purpose flour, 1 cup milk, 2 beaten eggs, 2 teaspoons sugar, and ½ teaspoon salt; beat with rotary beater till blended. Heat a lightly greased 6-inch skillet. Remove from heat; spoon in 2 tablespoons batter. Lift and tilt skillet to spread batter. Return to heat; brown on one side only. (*Or* cook on inverted crepe pan, see page 8.) Invert pan over paper toweling; remove crepe. Repeat to make 12 crepes, greasing skillet occasionally.

For filling: In skillet cook ½ pound fresh mushrooms, sliced, in 2 tablespoons butter *or* margarine till tender, about 5 minutes. Blend in 2 tablespoons all-purpose flour and ¾ teaspoon salt. Add 1 cup light cream all at once. Cook quickly, stirring constantly, till mixture is thickened and bubbly. Remove from heat; stir in 1 tablespoon dry sherry and 2 teaspoons lemon juice.

To assemble: Spoon 1 tablespoon filling along center of unbrowned side of each crepe. Fold opposite sides of each crepe so they overlap atop filling. Place crepes seam side down in 9x9x2-inch baking pan. Sprinkle with 2 tablespoons grated parmesan cheese and paprika. Dot with 2 tablespoons butter. Bake at 350° for 30 minutes. Serves 4 to 6.

Russian Buckwheat Blini

1 *cup buckwheat pancake mix*
1 *cup milk*
2 *beaten egg yolks*
1 *tablespoon butter, melted*

2 *stiffly beaten egg whites*
Caviar, butter, or *dairy*
   sour cream

For crepes: Combine pancake mix, milk, egg yolks, and butter; beat till blended. Fold in egg whites. Heat a lightly greased 6-inch skillet. Remove from heat; spoon in 1 tablespoon batter. Spread with spoon to make 4-inch circle. Return to heat; brown one side. Invert over paper toweling; remove crepe. Repeat to make 36 crepes, greasing pan occasionally.

To assemble: Spread caviar, butter, *or* sour cream over unbrowned side of crepe, leaving ¼-inch rim. Roll up as for jelly roll. Makes 36 crepes.

Chinese Mu-hsü-jou Crepes

1 cup all-purpose flour
1¼ cups water
2 beaten eggs
1 tablespoon sesame seed oil
   or cooking oil
¼ teaspoon salt
   • • •
½ pound boneless pork,
   cut ½ to ¾ inch
   thick
½ cup finely chopped green
   onion with tops
½ cup thinly sliced fresh
   mushrooms

¼ cup finely chopped
   celery
1 tablespoon sesame seed oil
   or cooking oil
   • • •
1 teaspoon cornstarch
1 teaspoon sugar
½ teaspoon salt
1 tablespoon dry sherry
1 tablespoon soy sauce
   • • •
4 beaten eggs
1 tablespoon milk

For crepes: In bowl combine flour, water, 2 beaten eggs, 1 tablespoon oil, and ¼ teaspoon salt; beat with rotary beater till blended. Heat a lightly greased 8-inch skillet. Remove from heat; spoon in a scant ¼ cup batter. Lift and tilt skillet to spread batter evenly. Return to heat; cook on one side only. (These will not be as brown as other crepes.) Invert pan over paper toweling. Remove crepe. Repeat with remaining batter to make 10 crepes, greasing pan occasionally.

For filling: Partially freeze pork. Cut in strips ¼ inch wide and 1 inch long. In skillet cook pork, green onion, mushrooms, and celery in 1 tablespoon hot oil till mushrooms and onions are tender, about 4 minutes. Combine cornstarch, sugar, and ½ teaspoon salt. Blend sherry and soy sauce into cornstarch mixture; stir into pork mixture. Cook and stir till thickened and bubbly. Combine 4 beaten eggs and milk; add to pork mixture. Turn heat to low. Don't disturb mixture till it starts to set on bottom and sides, then lift and fold over with wide spatula so uncooked part goes to bottom. Avoid breaking up eggs any more than necessary. Cook till eggs are cooked but still glossy and moist, about 5 minutes. Remove pork and egg mixture from heat immediately.

Meanwhile, reheat crepes between layers of foil on a foil-lined baking sheet, covered, at 375° about 7 minutes.

To assemble: Spoon about ¼ cup of the hot pork and egg filling in center of unbrowned side of each warm crepe. Fold two opposite edges of crepe so they overlap about 1 inch atop filling. Starting at unfolded edge roll crepe as for jelly roll, making sure folded sides are included in roll. Keep warm while rolling remaining crepes. Serve immediately. Traditionally, crepes are picked up and eaten. Makes 5 servings.

Savory Crepes Potpourri

Treat your guests to appetizers and snacks from this section. This fancy array includes *Harlequin Crepe Wedges, Salami Sandwich Cups, Gouda Crepe Roll-Ups* (all on platter), *Pigs-in-a-Blanket Crepes* (on warmer) and *Peanut-Crepe Nibble Mix* (see Index for pages).

Appetizers

Golden Swiss Crab Cups

16 Basic Main Dish Crepes
  (see recipe, page 11)
1 7½-ounce can crab meat,
  drained, flaked, and
  cartilage removed
1 cup shredded Swiss cheese
½ cup chopped water chestnuts

½ cup mayonnaise or salad
  dressing
1 tablespoon sliced green
  onion with tops
1 teaspoon lemon juice
¼ teaspoon curry powder
Snipped parsley

For crepe cups: Using a 2½-inch round cutter, cut three circles from each crepe. Carefully fit circles in greased 1¾-inch muffin pans.

To assemble: Combine crab, Swiss cheese, water chestnuts, mayonnaise, green onion, lemon juice, and curry powder; mix well. Spoon rounded teaspoon of filling into each cup. Bake at 400° till heated through, 10 to 12 minutes. Sprinkle with parsley. Makes 48 appetizers.

Gouda Crepe Roll-Ups

These cheese appetizers and the following three recipes are shown on pages 50-51—

For filling: Shred one 8-ounce package gouda *or* edam cheese to make about 2 cups; bring to room temperature. With electric mixer beat cheese at low speed till nearly smooth. Add ½ cup dairy sour cream and 1½ teaspoons Italian salad dressing mix. Beat till smooth and fluffy.

To assemble: Spread unbrowned side of 10 Parmesan Cheese Crepes (see recipe, page 13), with about 2½ tablespoons filling each. Cut each crepe into six wedges; roll each wedge as for jelly roll, starting at wide end. Serve at room temperature. Makes 60 appetizers.

Salami Sandwich Cups

12 Parmesan Cheese Crepes
  (see recipe, page 13)
1 cup shredded mozzarella cheese

¾ cup finely chopped salami
¾ cup finely chopped boiled ham
½ teaspoon caraway seed

For crepe cups: Using a 2½-inch round cutter, cut three circles from each crepe. Carefully fit circles in greased 1¾-inch muffin pans.

To assemble: Combine mozzarella, salami, ham, and caraway seed. Divide filling evenly among crepe cups. Bake, uncovered, at 400° till hot, about 10 to 12 minutes. Makes 36 appetizers.

Harlequin Crepe Wedges

1 cup ground fully cooked ham
⅓ cup finely chopped celery
½ cup mayonnaise or salad
   dressing
2 tablespoons drained pickle
   relish
1 teaspoon prepared horseradish
4 hard-cooked eggs, chopped
⅓ cup chopped pimiento-stuffed
   green olives
2 tablespoons finely chopped
   green onion with tops

2 teaspoons prepared mustard
⅛ teaspoon salt
   • • •
15 Whole Wheat or Basic
   Main Dish Crepes (see
   recipes, pages 14 and 11)
1 4-ounce container whipped
   cream cheese
  Green pepper strips
  Whole canned pimiento, sliced or
   cut in small
   designs

For fillings: Combine ham, celery, ¼ cup of the mayonnaise, relish, and horseradish; set aside. In separate bowl combine eggs, olives, onion, mustard, salt, and remaining mayonnaise or salad dressing; set aside.

To assemble: Spread unbrowned side of each of *10* of the crepes with about 2 tablespoons of either ham *or* egg filling. Make five stacks of 2 crepes each, filling side up. Top each stack with one of the remaining crepes, browned side up. Frost top of each stack with whipped cream cheese. Cut each into 6 wedges. Decorate tops with green pepper strips and pimiento. Cover and chill. Makes 30 appetizers.

Pigs-in-a-Blanket Crepes

10 Yellow Cornmeal Crepes
   (see recipe, page 13)
3 tablespoons Dijon-style
   mustard
50 cocktail frankfurters

¾ cup chili sauce
1 tablespoon lemon juice
2 teaspoons Worcestershire sauce
1 teaspoon prepared horseradish
¼ teaspoon onion salt

To assemble: Spread unbrowned side of each crepe with a scant teaspoon mustard. Cut each crepe into 5 strips. Place 1 cocktail frankfurter at one end of each strip. Roll up as for jelly roll. Arrange appetizers seam side down in a shallow baking pan. Bake at 425° till heated through, about 15 minutes. Serve immediately with sauce.

For sauce: In serving bowl combine chili sauce, lemon juice, Worcestershire sauce, horseradish, and onion salt. To serve spear appetizers with wooden picks and dip into horseradish sauce. Makes 50 appetizers.

Pineapple-Walnut Pinwheels

1 8-ounce package cream
  cheese, softened
½ cup finely chopped walnuts
⅓ cup pineapple preserves

2 tablespoons finely chopped
  candied ginger
8 Basic Dessert Crepes
  (see recipe, page 15)

For filling: Mix cream cheese, walnuts, preserves, and ginger.
To assemble: Spread 2 tablespoons filling over unbrowned side of each crepe; leave ¼-inch rim around edge. Roll up as for jelly roll; cut each crepe into six pieces. Place seam side down on plate. Makes 48.

Curried Cheese Rolls

1 8-ounce package neufchâtel or
  cream cheese, softened
2 tablespoons catsup
1½ teaspoons curry powder
1 teaspoon instant minced onion

1 teaspoon Worcestershire sauce
8 Basic Main Dish Crepes
  (see recipe, page 11)
¼ cup finely chopped peanuts
¼ cup chutney, finely chopped

For filling: In small mixing bowl combine cheese, catsup, curry, onion, and Worcestershire; beat at medium speed of electric mixer till fluffy.
To assemble: Spread unbrowned side of each crepe with about 2 tablespoons filling and sprinkle with about 1½ teaspoons peanuts. Cut each crepe into 6 wedges; spoon ¼ teaspoon chutney on each wedge. Roll each wedge as for jelly roll, starting at wide end. Serve at room temperature *or*, if desired, place seam side down on lightly greased baking sheet. Bake at 375° till heated through, 4 to 5 minutes. Makes 48.

Chili Pepper Crepe Cups

10 Yellow Cornmeal Crepes
  (see recipe, page 13)
1 cup shredded brick cheese

1 4-ounce can chili peppers,
  drained, seeded, and chopped
⅛ teaspoon garlic powder

For crepe cups: Using a 2½-inch round cutter, cut three circles from each crepe. Carefully fit circles in greased 1¾-inch muffin pans.
To assemble: Combine cheese, chili peppers, and garlic powder. Spoon about 2 teaspoons filling into each crepe cup. Bake at 400° till heated through, about 10 minutes. Makes 30 appetizers.

Horseradish Ham Rolls

3 tablespoons butter
1 teaspoon all-purpose flour
¼ cup vinegar
¼ cup beef broth
¼ cup prepared mustard
3 tablespoons brown sugar
1 tablespoon prepared horseradish

1 slightly beaten egg yolk
2 whole dill pickles
   (3½ to 4 inches long)
12 Whole Wheat Crepes
   (see recipe, page 14)
12 4-inch squares sliced boiled
   ham (9 ounces)

For sauce: In saucepan melt butter; blend in flour. Add vinegar, beef broth, mustard, sugar, and horseradish. Cook and stir till mixture thickens and bubbles. Slowly add half of the hot mixture to egg yolk; return to hot mixture. Bring to boiling; stir constantly. Remove from heat.

To assemble: Cut each pickle lengthwise into 6 pieces; set aside. Spread about 1 teaspoon sauce over unbrowned side of each crepe. Top with ham slice. Roll up around piece of pickle; trim ends. Cut each crepe into 6 slices. Place slices seam side down on greased 15x10x1-inch baking dish. Bake at 375° till hot, 10 to 12 minutes. Reheat sauce over *low* heat. Secure ham rolls with wooden pick; serve with sauce. Makes 72.

Avocado Meat Bundles

Yellow Cornmeal Crepes batter
   (see recipe, page 13)
1 4½-ounce can deviled ham or
   corned beef spread
½ cup shredded cheddar or
   monterey jack cheese

2 tablespoons chopped onion
1 tablespoon chopped pimiento
1 tablespoon lemon juice
¼ teaspoon salt
1 6-ounce carton frozen avocado
   dip, thawed

For crepes: Using 1 scant tablespoon batter for each, prepare 40 crepes by spooning batter into a hot lightly greased skillet or griddle and spreading with back of spoon into a 3-inch circle. (Cook 3 crepes at a time.) Brown on one side only, about 1 minute. Remove to paper toweling.

For filling: Combine deviled ham *or* corned beef spread with shredded cheese, onion, pimiento, lemon juice, and salt.

To assemble: Spoon 1 teaspoon filling mixture slightly off-center of unbrowned side of crepe; fold in half. Moisten edges with water; press edges with tines of fork to seal. Place on ungreased baking sheet; repeat with remaining crepes. Bake at 425° till golden, about 10 minutes. Top with spoonful of avocado dip. Makes 40 appetizers.

Blue Cheese Paté Crepes

1 4-*ounce container whipped cream cheese*
¼ *cup crumbled blue cheese*
½ *of a 4¾-ounce can liver spread*
1 *tablespoon dry sherry*
¼ *cup chopped water chestnuts*

2 *slices bacon, crisp-cooked, drained, and crumbled*
1 *tablespoon finely chopped onion*
8 *Basic Main Dish Crepes (see recipe, page 11)*
48 *pimiento-stuffed green olives*

For filling: In small bowl blend together cheeses, liver spread, and sherry. Stir in water chestnuts, bacon, and onion.
To assemble: Spread 2 to 3 tablespoons filling over unbrowned side of each crepe. Cut each into 6 wedges; roll up as for jelly roll, beginning at wide end. Skewer an olive with each on wooden pick. Makes 48.

Cheesy Shrimp Snacks

36 *Crepe Chips (see page 16)*
1 *5-ounce jar neufchâtel cheese spread with pineapple*

1 *4½-ounce can small shrimp, drained*

To assemble: On baking sheet dollop each chip with 1 teaspoon cheese; top with 2 shrimp. Bake at 375° till hot, about 7 minutes. Makes 36.

Salmon Appetizer Cornucopias

Basic Main Dish Crepes batter (see recipe, page 11)
1 16-*ounce can salmon, drained, boned, and flaked*

½ *cup mayonnaise or salad dressing*
1 *teaspoon prepared mustard*
2 *tablespoons capers, drained*

For crepes: Using 1 scant tablespoon batter for each crepe, prepare 48 crepes by spooning batter into a hot lightly greased skillet or griddle and spreading with back of spoon into a 3-inch circle. (Cook 3 crepes at a time.) Brown on one side only; remove to paper toweling.
For filling: Combine the salmon, mayonnaise, and mustard.
To assemble: Spread 2 teaspoons filling over unbrowned side of each crepe. Roll into cornucopias; place seam side down on serving plate. Trim with capers. Cover; chill till serving time. Makes 48.

Snacks

Peanut-Crepe Nibble Mix

Serve this crunchy snack, shown on pages 50-51, at a party or for snacking anytime–

5 *tablespoons butter or*
 margarine
2 *tablespoons Italian salad*
 dressing mix

5 *cups puffed oat cereal*
3 *cups Crepe Noodles (see*
 recipe, page 16)
2 *cups Spanish peanuts*

In a 13x9x2-inch baking pan melt butter *or* margarine in a 300° oven, 3 to 4 minutes. Remove from oven. Blend in Italian salad dressing mix. Add oat cereal, tossing to coat thoroughly. Add Crepe Noodles and peanuts, stirring gently. Return to oven and heat 15 minutes longer. Cool nibble mix before serving. Makes about 10 cups.

Curry-Crepe Nibble Mix

¼ *cup butter* or *margarine*
1 *to* 1½ *teaspoons curry powder*
¼ *teaspoon onion salt*
¼ *teaspoon ground ginger*

2 *cups tiny pretzels*
2 *cups Crepe Noodles (see*
 recipe, page 16)
1½ *cups cheese croutons*

In a large skillet melt butter. Blend in curry powder, onion salt, and ginger. Add pretzels, Crepe Noodles, and croutons. Toss to coat. Heat 15 minutes over low heat, stirring frequently. Cool. Makes 5½ cups.

Creamy Cheese Fondue

4 *cups shredded American cheese*
 (16 ounces)
1 *tablespoon all-purpose flour*
2 *tablespoons finely chopped*
 green pepper
1 *tablespoon butter*

1 *cup dry white wine*
2 *3-ounce packages cream*
 cheese with chives
1 *teaspoon prepared mustard*
 Crepe Chips (see recipe,
 page 16)

Toss American cheese with flour to coat; set aside. In saucepan cook green pepper in butter till tender but not brown. Stir in wine; heat slowly just till bubbly. Gradually add shredded cheese, stirring constantly till smooth and bubbly. Stir in cream cheese and mustard; cook and stir over low heat till smooth. Transfer to fondue pot; place over fondue burner. Dip Crepe Chips in fondue. Makes about 3½ cups.

Hot Chili-Bean Dipper

1 16-ounce can refried beans
1 11-ounce can condensed
    cheddar cheese soup
¼ cup milk

3 tablespoons finely chopped
    canned green chili peppers
    Crepe Chips (see recipe,
    page 16)

In saucepan combine beans, soup, milk, and chili peppers. Heat slowly, stirring constantly, till smooth and bubbly. Transfer to fondue pot; place over fondue burner. Dip Crepe Chips in fondue. Makes 3 cups.

Braunschweiger Chip Dip

With an electric mixer beat together 8 ounces braunschweiger, one 8-ounce carton sour cream dip with French onion, ¼ cup finely chopped dill pickle, 1 tablespoon milk, 1½ teaspoons prepared mustard, and ⅛ teaspoon bottled hot pepper sauce till blended. Cover and chill. Serve with Crepe Chips (see recipe, page 16). Makes about 4 cups.

Green Goddess Chip Dip

¾ cup mayonnaise
¾ cup dairy sour cream
¼ cup snipped parsley
2 tablespoons snipped chives

1 tablespoon anchovy paste
1 teaspoon lemon juice
1 small clove garlic, minced
    Crepe Chips (see page 16)

Combine mayonnaise, sour cream, parsley, chives, anchovy paste, lemon juice, and garlic. Chill. Garnish with additional snipped chives, if desired. Serve with Crepe Chips. Makes about 1½ cups dip.

Shallow-Fat Frying Use a heavy saucepan or skillet at least 3 inches deep to allow for a sufficient depth of cooking oil. Monitor temperature of fat with a deep-fat thermometer. Or, check temperature by adding a 1-inch cube of bread —if it browns in 1 minute, fat is hot enough. Add only a few pieces of food at a time to keep fat from cooling too quickly. Drain fried food on paper toweling. Cool fat after frying, then strain it to remove crumbs. Cover; chill for later use.

Sandwiches

Breakfast Sandwich Bundles

For filling: Brown 10 brown-and-serve sausage links according to package directions; drain. Cut each in half lengthwise. In bowl combine 1½ cups chunk-style applesauce and ¼ teaspoon ground cinnamon.

To assemble: Using 10 Pancake Mix Crepes (see recipe, page 14), place 2 sausage halves in center of unbrowned side of each crepe; top with 2 tablespoons applesauce mixture. Overlap two opposite edges of crepe atop filling; fold in remaining edges forming a square packet. Place seam side down in 12x7½x2-inch baking dish. Bake at 375° till hot, about 15 minutes. Pass warmed maple syrup. Makes 5 servings.

Calorie Counter's Special

1 cup cream-style cottage cheese with chives	⅛ teaspoon pepper Leaf lettuce or fresh spinach
2 medium carrots, shredded	8 Calorie Counter's Crepes
2 medium tomatoes, chopped	(see recipe, page 11)
½ teaspoon salt	Low-calorie French-style
¼ teaspoon dried basil, crushed	salad dressing

For filling: Combine cheese, carrots, tomatoes, and seasonings.

To assemble: Place a piece of lettuce on unbrowned side of each crepe. Spread with about 2 tablespoons filling. Fold two opposite edges of each crepe so they overlap atop filling. Pass dressing. Serves 4.

Reuben Sandwich Crepes

1 16-ounce can sauerkraut, rinsed and snipped	16 Whole Wheat Crepes (see recipe, page 14)
½ teaspoon caraway seed	⅓ cup Thousand Island salad
2 3- or 4-ounce packages thinly sliced corned beef	dressing
	8 slices Swiss cheese, quartered

For filling: Combine snipped sauerkraut and caraway seed.

To assemble: Place 2 or 3 slices meat on unbrowned side of each crepe; top with 2 tablespoons filling and 1 teaspoon dressing. Overlap 2 opposite edges of crepe atop filling. Place seam side down on baking sheet. Bake at 375°, covered, till hot, about 20 minutes. Top each crepe with 2 cheese quarters; bake till cheese melts. Makes 8 servings.

Danish Sandwich Crepes

12 *Yellow Cornmeal Crepes*
   (see recipe, page 13)
   Mayonnaise or *salad dressing*
1 *3- or 4-ounce package*
   thinly sliced turkey

Finely shredded lettuce
8 *ounces sliced pastrami*
6 *slices Swiss cheese, halved*
2 *or 3 medium dill pickles,*
   sliced

To assemble: Spread unbrowned side of 6 crepes with mayonnaise or salad dressing. Arrange on baking sheet, mayonnaise side up. Top with *half* the turkey, lettuce, pastrami, cheese, and pickles. Repeat layers *exept* spread *browned* side of remaining 6 crepes with mayonnaise. Bake at 350° till cheese melts slightly, 10 to 12 minutes. Makes 6 servings.

Cheeseburger Crepes

1 *pound ground beef*
¼ *cup finely chopped onion*
1 *tablespoon prepared mustard*
1 *tablespoon sweet pickle relish*
¾ *teaspoon salt*
¼ *teaspoon pepper*

1 *cup shredded American*
   cheese (4 ounces)
16 *Basic Main Dish Crepes*
   (see recipe, page 11)
2 *tomatoes, seeded and chopped*
1 *cup catsup*

For filling: In skillet cook beef and onion till beef is browned, drain fat. Stir in mustard, relish, salt, and pepper. Stir in cheese.
To assemble: Spoon 3 tablespoons filling along center of unbrowned side of crepe. Top with some tomato. Fold 2 opposite edges of crepe so they overlap atop filling; place *seam side up* in greased 15½x10½x1-inch baking pan. Repeat with remaining crepes. Bake, covered, at 375° for 25 minutes. Spoon catsup atop each; bake, uncovered, 5 minutes. Makes 8 servings.

Bologna Sandwich Crepes

To assemble: Using 12 slices bologna and 12 Whole Wheat Crepes (see recipe, page 14), lay 1 slice bologna on unbrowned side of each crepe. Roll up as for jelly roll. Place seam side down in 12x7½x2-inch baking dish. Bake, covered, at 375° for 15 to 20 minutes.
For Mustard Sauce: In saucepan heat together ½ cup dairy sour cream, ½ cup mayonnaise, and 1 tablespoon prepared mustard. Spoon over crepes; sprinkle with ½ cup shredded cheddar cheese. Makes 6 servings.

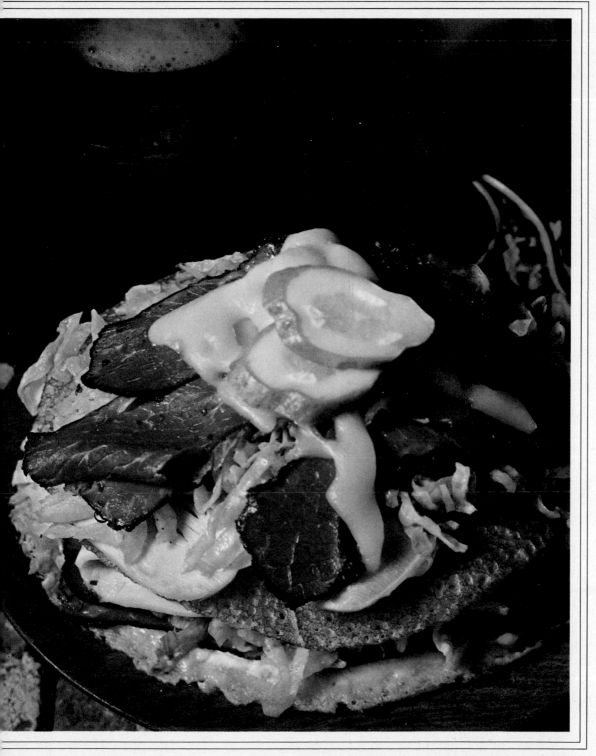

No one will go hungry when you serve *Danish Sandwich Crepes*.
Stack cornmeal crepes with turkey, pastrami, and Swiss
cheese to make this double-decker, knife-and-fork sandwich.

Vegetables

Ratatouille-Filled Crepes

You'll love this Mediterranean-style vegetable combination shown on page 4—

1 *medium onion, thinly sliced*
1 *medium green pepper, chopped*
1 *clove garlic, minced*
2 *tablespoons cooking oil*
3½ *cups cubed, peeled eggplant*
1 *small zucchini, sliced (1 cup)*
1 *16-ounce can tomatoes, cut up*

1 *tablespoon snipped parsley*
1 *teaspoon salt*
1 *teaspoon dried basil, crushed*
½ *teaspoon sugar*
⅛ *teaspoon pepper*
12 *Basic Main Dish Crepes*
   (see recipe, page 11)

For filling: In large skillet cook onion, green pepper, and garlic in oil till tender. Add eggplant and zucchini; cook and stir for 4 to 5 minutes. Stir in tomatoes, parsley, and seasonings. Simmer, uncovered, till vegetables are tender, 15 to 20 minutes, stirring occasionally.

To assemble: Spoon ¼ cup filling along center of unbrowned side of crepe. Fold 2 opposite edges of crepe so they overlap atop filling. Place seam side down in 12x7½x2-inch baking dish. Repeat with remaining crepes. Bake, uncovered, at 375° about 20 minutes. Top with dairy sour cream *or* yogurt, if desired. Makes 6 servings.

Broccoli-Cheese Crepes

1 *10-ounce package frozen cut*
   broccoli
1 *3-ounce can sliced mushrooms*
1 *tablespoon butter*
1 *tablespoon all-purpose flour*
¼ *teaspoon salt*
¾ *cup milk*

¾ *cup shredded process Swiss*
   cheese (3 ounces)
2 *tablespoons chopped pimiento*
10 *Basic Main Dish Crepes*
   (see recipe, page 11)
½ *cup soft bread crumbs*
1 *tablespoon butter, melted*

For filling: Cook broccoli according to package directions; drain well. Drain mushrooms, reserving liquid. In saucepan melt 1 tablespoon butter; blend in flour and salt. Add milk and reserved mushroom liquid all at once. Cook and stir till thickened and bubbly. Stir in ½ *cup* of the cheese till melted. Stir in broccoli, mushrooms, and pimiento.

To assemble: Spoon ¼ cup filling along center of unbrowned side of each crepe. Overlap 2 opposite edges atop filling. Place seam side down in 13x 9x2-inch baking dish. Bake, covered, at 375° for 15 minutes. Combine crumbs, remaining ¼ cup cheese, and melted butter. Sprinkle atop crepes. Bake, uncovered, 5 minutes more. Makes 5 servings.

Sherry-Sauced Mushroom Crepes

8 ounces fresh mushrooms,
  coarsely chopped
¼ cup butter or margarine
12 Basic Main Dish Crepes
  (see recipe, page 11)

1 cup light cream
1 tablespoon all-purpose flour
2 tablespoons dry sherry
  Dash ground nutmeg
2 beaten egg yolks

For filling: Cook mushrooms in butter till tender, about 5 minutes.
To assemble: Spoon 3 tablespoons filling along center of unbrowned side of each crepe; overlap two opposite edges atop filling. Place seam side down in 13x9x2-inch baking dish. Bake, covered, at 375° for 15 minutes.
For Sherry Sauce: In small saucepan blend cream into flour; stir in sherry, nutmeg, and ¼ teaspoon salt. Cook and stir till slightly thickened and bubbly. Slowly stir into yolks; return to pan. Cook and stir till thickened and almost boiling, about 2 minutes. *Do not overcook.* Spoon over crepes; top with snipped parsley, if desired. Makes 6 servings.

Greek-Style Spinach Tarts

For filling: Cook ½ cup chopped onion in ¼ cup butter. Blend in ¼ cup all-purpose flour, ½ teaspoon dried dillweed, and ½ teaspoon salt. Add 1½ cups milk; cook and stir till bubbly. Remove from heat. Stir *half* into 3 beaten eggs; return to pan. Add 1 cup cream-style cottage cheese; stir in one 10-ounce package frozen chopped spinach, cooked and drained.
To assemble: Using 24 Parmesan Cheese Crepes (see page 13), place 2 crepes, unbrowned sides together, in each of 12 greased 6-ounce custard cups. Arrange ruffled tops. Spoon ⅓ cup filling into each. Bake at 350° till set, 30 to 35 minutes. Let stand 5 minutes. Makes 12 servings.

Crepe Noodle-Vegetable Soup

Peel and cut into julienne strips 2 carrots, 1 potato, and 1 small turnip. In saucepan combine vegetables with 6 cups water; 1 small onion, cut in thin wedges; 3 tablespoons instant beef bouillon granules; 1 teaspoon dried marjoram, crushed; ¼ teaspoon salt; and dash pepper. Bring to boiling; cover and simmer till vegetables are tender, 15 minutes. Add 2 cups coarsely shredded fresh spinach; cook 5 minutes more. Cut 4 to 6 Parmesan Cheese Crepes *or* Basic Main Dish Crepes (see pages 13 and 11) into ¼-inch strips with sharp knife. Add to soup; heat 1 minute. Serves 8.

Distinctive Dessert Crepes

If you crave sweets, the recipes in this section are for you. Choose from chocolate or fruit crepes, flaming desserts, and crepes with ice cream. The crepes pictured here are sure to be among your favorites. They include *Lemon Meringue Crepes* (see recipe, page 70), *Summer Fruit Crepe Cups* (see recipe, page 66), and *Fruit Crepe Strudels* (see recipe, page 67).

Dessert magic

Chocolate Éclair Crepes

⅓ cup sugar
1 tablespoon all-purpose flour
1 tablespoon cornstarch
1½ cups milk
1 slightly beaten egg yolk
1 teaspoon vanilla
½ cup whipping cream
12 Fluffy All-Purpose Crepes
　(see recipe, page 13)

½ cup sugar
4 teaspoons cornstarch
½ cup water
1 1-ounce square unsweetened
　chocolate, chopped
　Dash salt
1 tablespoon butter
　or margarine
½ teaspoon vanilla

For filling: In saucepan combine ⅓ cup sugar, flour, 1 tablespoon cornstarch, and ¼ teaspoon salt. Slowly stir in milk. Cook and stir till bubbly; cook and stir 2 to 3 minutes more. Stir *half* into egg yolk; return to saucepan. Cook and stir just till bubbly. Add 1 teaspoon vanilla; cool. Beat smooth. Whip cream till soft peaks form; fold into filling.

To assemble: Spoon 3 tablespoons filling along center of unbrowned side of each crepe. Fold two opposite edges so they overlap atop filling. With wide spatula, transfer to baking sheet. Chill.

For Chocolate Glaze: In saucepan combine ½ cup sugar and 4 teaspoons cornstarch. Add water, chocolate, and dash salt. Cook and stir till thickened and bubbly. Remove from heat; stir in butter and ½ teaspoon vanilla. While hot, spread over crepes. Chill. Makes 12 servings.

Summer Fruit Crepe Cups

See this fresh-as-summer dessert treat on pages 64-65–

2 cups fresh or frozen blue-
　berries or blackberries
1 cup fresh strawberries, halved
2 medium bananas
1 cup cantaloupe or honeydew
　melon balls

2 teaspoons lemon juice
1 8-ounce carton orange yogurt
2 tablespoons sugar
10 Oven-Baked Crepe Cups
　(see recipe, page 16)
　Toasted coconut

For filling: Remove stems from berries. Bias-slice bananas. Combine fruits; sprinkle with lemon juice to prevent darkening.

For sauce: Stir together orange yogurt and sugar.

To assemble: Set crepe cups in dessert dishes. Fill each with about ¼ cup fruit filling. Top with the yogurt sauce; add the remaining fruit filling. Sprinkle with toasted coconut. Makes 10 servings.

Fruit Crepe Strudels

Sugar and cinnamon make these fruit-filled crepes, shown on pages 64-65, crispy on top–

1 cup all-purpose flour
1½ cups milk
2 eggs
1 tablespoon cooking oil
¼ teaspoon salt
• • •
1 20- to 24-ounce can fruit pie
   filling (apple, cherry,
   apricot, raisin, mincemeat,
   peach, or blueberry)

½ cup finely chopped toasted
   nuts
½ teaspoon grated lemon peel
½ teaspoon vanilla
½ cup butter or margarine,
   melted
6 tablespoons fine dry bread
   crumbs
1 tablespoon sugar
¼ teaspoon ground cinnamon

For crepes: In bowl combine flour, milk, eggs, oil, and salt; beat with rotary beater till blended. Heat a lightly greased 10-inch skillet; remove from heat. Pour in about ⅓ cup batter; lift and tilt skillet to spread batter evenly. Return to heat; brown on one side only. To remove, invert pan over paper toweling; remove crepe. Repeat with remaining batter to make 6 crepes, greasing pan occasionally.

For filling: Combine pie filling, nuts, lemon peel, and vanilla.

To assemble: Brush unbrowned side of each crepe with about 1 tablespoon melted butter; sprinkle with 1 tablespoon bread crumbs. Spoon a scant ½ cup filling at one end of each crepe. Roll up as for jelly roll, starting with filling end. Fold sides under. Place crepes seam side down on lightly greased baking sheet. Brush with remaining melted butter. Combine sugar and cinnamon; sprinkle atop. Bake at 400° till crispy, about 15 minutes. Let stand 5 minutes; cut in pieces. Serves 12.

Miniature Pecan Crepe Cups

8 Basic Dessert Crepes
   (see recipe, page 15)
1 egg
¾ cup packed brown sugar

1 tablespoon butter, melted
1 teaspoon vanilla
Dash salt
½ cup chopped pecans

For crepe cups: Using 2½-inch round cutter, cut three circles from each crepe. Carefully fit circles in greased 1¾-inch muffin pans.

For filling: Beat egg with brown sugar, butter, vanilla, and salt.

To assemble: Place about 1 teaspoon pecans in each cup; top with about 1½ teaspoons filling. Bake at 350° for 20 minutes. Makes 24.

When you want a scrumptious do-ahead dessert, remember *Red Raspberry Crepes*. Chill the cream cheese-filled crepes and the *Raspberry Sauce* separately, then combine and heat to serve.

Red Raspberry Crepes

1 4-ounce container whipped
   cream cheese, softened
10 Basic Dessert Crepes
   (see recipe, page 15)
⅓ cup toasted slivered almonds
1 10-ounce package frozen red
   raspberries, thawed
   Cranberry juice cocktail

⅓ cup sugar
4 teaspoons cornstarch
   Dash salt
2 tablespoons butter
   or margarine
2 tablespoons orange liqueur
   (optional)
2 teaspoons lemon juice

To assemble: Spread cream cheese over unbrowned side of crepe, leaving ¼-inch rim around edge. Sprinkle with some of the almonds. Roll up as for jelly roll. Repeat with remaining crepes. Reserve remaining almonds for garnish. Cover crepes and chill.

For Raspberry Sauce: Drain berries; reserve syrup. Add cranberry juice to syrup to make 1½ cups. Combine sugar, cornstarch, and salt. Blend in syrup mixture. Cook and stir till bubbly. Add butter, liqueur, lemon juice, and berries. Keep warm, *or* chill and heat before serving.

To serve: Arrange crepes in chafing dish or skillet; add hot sauce. Cover; heat through. Sprinkle with reserved almonds. Makes 5 servings.

Peachy Pecan Crepes

See this combination of peaches, cheese-filled crepes, and orange sauce shown on page 2–

2 3-ounce packages cream cheese,
   softened
3 tablespoons sugar
2 tablespoons milk
½ teaspoon grated orange peel
¼ teaspoon vanilla
16 Basic Dessert Crepes
   (see recipe, page 15)

¼ cup finely chopped pecans
1 29-ounce can peach slices
2 tablespoons cornstarch
½ cup orange juice
2 tablespoons lemon juice
2 tablespoons butter
   or margarine

For filling: Blend cream cheese, sugar, milk, orange peel, and vanilla.

To assemble: Spoon filling in center of unbrowned side of crepe; sprinkle with pecans. Fold crepe in half; fold in half again, forming a triangle. Repeat with remaining crepes. Drain peach slices; reserve syrup. In chafing dish or skillet blend syrup into cornstarch. Add orange juice, lemon juice, and butter. Cook and stir till thickened and bubbly. Add peaches and crepes. Spoon sauce over; heat through. Makes 8 servings.

Lemon Meringue Crepes

Lemon lovers will rave about this stacked version of the popular pie shown on pages 64-65–

1¾ cups sugar
3 tablespoons cornstarch
3 tablespoons all-purpose flour
1½ cups water
2 egg yolks
1 egg
2 tablespoons butter

½ teaspoon grated lemon peel
⅓ cup lemon juice
12 *Basic Dessert Crepes*
   (see recipe, page 15)
2 egg whites
½ teaspoon vanilla
¼ teaspoon cream of tartar

For Lemon Filling: In saucepan combine 1½ cups of the sugar, corn-starch, flour, and dash salt; stir in water. Cook and stir over high heat till boiling. Reduce heat; cook and stir 2 minutes more. Slightly beat egg yolks and egg. Stir in *1 cup* hot mixture; immediately return to saucepan. Bring to boiling; cook 2 minutes, stirring constantly. Remove from heat. Add butter and lemon peel. Slowly stir in lemon juice; pour into bowl. Place clear plastic wrap or waxed paper directly on top of filling; smooth paper to touch side of bowl. Cool, then chill.

To assemble: Place 1 crepe browned side down on foil-lined baking sheet. Spread with ¼ cup filling. Layer crepes, *browned side up,* and filling 4 more times ending with filling. Top with a crepe. Repeat for second stack.

For Meringue Topping: In mixing bowl beat egg whites, vanilla, and cream of tartar with electric mixer till soft peaks form. Gradually add re-maining ¼ cup sugar; beat till stiff and glossy peaks form. Spread or pipe on top of each stack. Broil 4 or 5 inches from heat till golden, 1 to 2 minutes. Serve at once or chill. Makes 8 servings.

Low-Calorie Cherry Crepes

For sauce: In saucepan mix ¼ cup sugar, 1 tablespoon cornstarch, and 1 teaspoon grated orange peel. Stir in 1 cup low-calorie cranberry juice cocktail. Add one 20-ounce can pitted tart red cherries (water pack), drained, and few drops red food coloring. Cook and stir till bubbly.

For filling: Combine ½ cup low-calorie imitation sour cream (*or* ½ cup yogurt mixed with 2 teaspoons sugar), 1 tablespoon sugar, and ⅛ tea-spoon ground cinnamon.

To assemble: Using 16 Calorie Counter's Crepes (see recipe, page 11), spread filling over unbrowned side of each crepe, leaving ¼-inch rim around edge. Roll up as for jelly roll. Place seam side down in chafing dish or skillet. Pour sauce over; heat through. Makes 8 servings.

Chocolate Mint Patty Stacks

½ cup all-purpose flour
½ cup milk
3 eggs, separated
¼ cup sugar
3 tablespoons butter, melted
¼ teaspoon vanilla

½ cup whipping cream
½ cup fudge topping
2 teaspoons white crème de menthe
2 teaspoons crème de cacao
Toasted sliced almonds

For Mini Crepes: In a bowl combine flour, milk, egg yolks, sugar, butter, and vanilla; beat with rotary beater till blended. In large bowl beat egg whites till stiff peaks form. Fold batter into egg whites. Heat a lightly greased 6-inch skillet; remove from heat. Spoon in 1 tablespoon batter; spread with back of spoon to 4-inch circle. Return to heat. Brown on one side only. Invert over paper toweling; remove crepe. Repeat with remaining batter to make 24 crepes, greasing pan occasionally.

For filling: Whip cream to soft peaks. Blend together fudge topping and liqueurs; fold whipped cream into fudge mixture.

To assemble: Place 1 crepe browned side down on plate. Spread with 1 tablespoon filling. Repeat layers 3 times more, layering crepes *browned side up* and ending with filling. Make 6 stacks. Sprinkle with nuts. Serves 6.

Cherry and Pecan Cones

For filling: Whip 1 cup whipping cream with ½ cup sugar to soft peaks. Fold in 1 cup dairy sour cream and ½ cup toasted chopped pecans.

To assemble: Using 24 Mini Crepes (see recipe, above), spoon 2 tablespoons filling on unbrowned side of each crepe. Roll into cone. Spoon 1 teaspoon cherry preserves in open end of each cone. Makes 24.

Brandied Apple Roll-Ups

For filling: In saucepan combine ¼ cup sugar and 1 tablespoon cornstarch. Stir in 1 cup chunk-style applesauce. Cook, stirring constantly, till thickened and bubbly; stir in ¼ cup brandy.

To assemble: Using 24 Mini Crepes (see above), spread 1 tablespoon filling over unbrowned side of each crepe, leaving ¼-inch rim around edge. Roll up as for jelly roll. Place seam side down in greased 15½x10½x1-inch baking pan. Bake, covered, at 350° for 10 minutes. Mix ¼ cup sugar and 1 teaspoon ground cinnamon; sprinkle over crepes. Makes 24.

Strawberry Shortcake Stacks

For filling: Blend ½ cup strawberry preserves and 4 teaspoons orange liqueur. Cut 1 quart strawberries in ¼-inch slices, reserving 6 whole strawberries for garnish. Whip 1½ cups whipping cream to soft peaks.

To assemble: Using 10 Basic Dessert Crepes (see recipe, page 15), place 1 crepe browned side down on serving platter; spread with 1 tablespoon preserve mixture. Then spread with about ¼ cup whipped cream. Arrange about ⅓ cup berries over cream. Repeat layering crepes, *browned side up* along with preserves, whipped cream, and strawberries 3 times more. Top with a crepe browned side up. Repeat to make a second stack. Center 3 of the reserved berries atop of each of the stacks. Pipe remaining whipped cream around edge of the top of each stack. Chill stacks, if desired. Cut each stack into 6 wedges. Makes 12 servings.

Butterscotch-Sauced Crepes

For filling: In mixing bowl beat ¼ cup sifted powdered sugar; one 3-ounce package cream cheese, softened; and ¼ teaspoon vanilla.

To assemble: Using 10 Spicy Dessert Crepes (see recipe, page 15), spoon about 1 tablespoon filling in center of unbrowned side of crepe. Sprinkle with about 1 tablespoon chopped walnuts. Fold crepe in half; fold in half again, forming a triangle. Repeat with remaining crepes.

For Butterscotch Sauce: In chafing dish or skillet combine ½ cup packed brown sugar, ¼ cup light corn syrup, ¼ cup milk, and 2 tablespoons butter. Bring to boiling. Add crepes; simmer till heated through, 5 to 7 minutes. Spoon sauce over crepes as they heat. Makes 10 servings.

Peanut Butter-Banana Boats

For filling: Quarter 3 medium bananas lengthwise. Coat banana pieces with 1 teaspoon lemon juice.

To assemble: Using 12 Basic Dessert Crepes (see recipe, page 15), place a banana quarter on unbrowned side of crepe. Roll up as for jelly roll. Place seam side down in 13x9x2-inch baking dish. Repeat with remaining crepes. Bake, covered, at 375° for 15 minutes.

For sauce: In saucepan combine ¾ cup milk, ½ cup semisweet chocolate pieces, and ¼ cup peanut butter. Cook, stirring constantly, till chocolate melts and sauce is smooth. Spoon over each serving of crepes. Sprinkle with ¼ cup chopped peanuts. Makes 6 servings.

When it comes to interesting flavor combinations, you can't top *Grape-Syruped Crepes*. Heat these delicate cream cheese- and pecan-filled lemon crepes in the tasty grape sauce, and sprinkle them with grated lemon peel, if desired.

Grape-Syruped Crepes

1 *4-ounce container whipped*
   cream cheese
12 *Lemon Dessert Crepes*
   (see recipe, page 16)
⅓ *cup chopped pecans*

1 *6-ounce can frozen grape*
   juice concentrate, thawed
4 *teaspoons cornstarch*
2 *tablespoons sugar*
1 *teaspoon grated lemon peel*

To assemble: Spread cream cheese over unbrowned side of crepe, leaving ¼-inch rim around edge. Sprinkle with nuts. Roll up as for jelly roll. Repeat with remaining crepes. In chafing dish or skillet stir grape juice into cornstarch; add ½ cup water. Cook and stir till sauce is thickened and bubbly. Stir in sugar and lemon peel. Add crepes; heat through, spooning sauce over crepes. Makes 6 servings.

Grasshopper Crepes

For filling: Chill ¼ cup green crème de menthe and ¼ cup white crème de cacao. In mixing bowl combine two 1½-ounce packages dessert topping mix and ⅔ cup milk. Prepare according to package directions. Chill 10 minutes. Gradually fold in chilled crème de menthe and white crème de cacao. Reserve ¾ cup; cover and chill.

To assemble: Using remaining filling and 16 Chocolate Dessert Crepes (see recipe, page 15), spoon about 2 tablespoons filling along center of unbrowned side of each crepe. Fold two opposite edges of each crepe so they overlap atop filling; cover and chill. Just before serving thin the reserved filling with 1 or 2 tablespoons milk. Spoon over crepes. Garnish with chocolate curls. Makes 8 servings.

Harvey Wallbanger Crepes

½ cup granulated sugar
⅓ cup orange juice
⅓ cup Galliano
2 tablespoons vodka

2 tablespoons butter
16 Basic Dessert Crepes (see recipe, page 15)
Sifted powdered sugar

For sauce: In 10-inch skillet *or* chafing dish, combine sugar, orange juice, Galliano, vodka, and butter. Heat till bubbly.

To assemble: Sprinkle unbrowned side of crepe with about 1 teaspoon powdered sugar. Fold crepe in half; fold in half again, forming a triangle. Repeat with remaining crepes; arrange in sauce. Simmer till sauce thickens slightly, 8 to 10 minutes, spooning sauce over crepes frequently. Serves 8.

Daiquiri-Filled Crepes

For filling: Prepare Lime Filling (see recipe, page 19), *except* reduce water to ½ cup. Stir in ¼ cup rum. Cover surface with clear plastic wrap. Cool without stirring. In mixing bowl beat 2 egg whites with ¼ teaspoon cream of tartar till stiff peaks form. Fold in filling.

To assemble: Using 16 Basic Dessert Crepes (see recipe, page 15), spread about 2 tablespoons filling over unbrowned side of crepe, leaving ¼-inch rim around edge. Roll up as for jelly roll. Repeat with remaining crepes. Cover and chill *or* serve immediately. Just before serving sprinkle with sifted powdered sugar and garnish with lime slices. Makes 8 servings.

Orange-Chocolate Crepes

1 cup granulated sugar
¼ cup cornstarch
1½ teaspoons grated orange peel
   (set aside)
1 cup orange juice
¼ cup butter or margarine
1 tablespoon lemon juice

12 Basic Dessert Crepes (see
   recipe, page 15)
1 1-ounce square unsweetened
   chocolate
1½ cups sifted powdered sugar
1 teaspoon vanilla
   Boiling water

For filling: Mix 1 cup sugar, cornstarch, and ½ teaspoon salt. Add orange juice. Cook and stir till thickened. Stir in *2 tablespoons* butter, lemon juice, and orange peel; cover surface with plastic wrap. Cool without stirring.
To assemble: Spread about 2 tablespoons filling over unbrowned side of crepe, leaving ¼-inch rim around edge. Roll up as for jelly roll. Place seam side down on waxed paper. Repeat with remaining crepes.
For glaze: Melt chocolate and remaining 2 tablespoons butter over low heat, stirring constantly. Remove from heat. Stir in powdered sugar and vanilla till crumbly. Blend in 3 tablespoons boiling water. Add about 1 tablespoon more boiling water, a teaspoon at a time, till glaze is pouring consistency. Drizzle about 1 tablespoon over each crepe; chill. Makes 12.

Rich Cannoli Crepes

¾ cup sugar
3 tablespoons cornstarch
¾ cup milk
1 pound ricotta cheese
1½ teaspoons vanilla
½ cup semisweet chocolate
   pieces, coarsely chopped

2 tablespoons finely chopped
   candied citron
12 Basic Dessert Crepes (see
   recipe, page 15)
   Sweetened whipped cream
2 tablespoons finely chopped
   pistachio nuts

For filling: In saucepan mix sugar and cornstarch; blend in milk. Cook and stir till thickened; cook 1 minute more. Cover surface with clear plastic wrap or waxed paper; cool without stirring. With electric mixer beat ricotta and vanilla till creamy; blend in cornstarch mixture. Stir in chocolate and citron. Cover; chill.
To assemble: Spoon ¼ cup filling along center of unbrowned side of each crepe. Fold two opposite edges of each crepe so they overlap atop filling. Place seam side down in dessert dish. Top with whipped cream and nuts. (If desired, tint nuts green with food coloring.) Makes 12 servings.

Lemon Cheesecake Crepes

½ recipe Lemon Dessert Crepes
  batter (see recipe, page 16)
¼ cup sugar
1 teaspoon unflavored gelatin
¼ teaspoon salt
2 3-ounce packages cream cheese,
  softened

½ cup lemon yogurt
¼ teaspoon grated lemon peel
1 tablespoon lemon juice
  Few drops yellow food coloring
½ cup frozen whipped dessert
  topping, thawed
⅔ cup red raspberry preserves

For crepes: Using 1½ tablespoons batter for each, prepare 10 crepes by spooning batter into large skillet or griddle and spreading with back of spoon to make a 4-inch circle. (Cook several crepes at a time.) Brown on one side only. Invert on paper toweling; remove crepes.

For filling: In saucepan combine sugar, gelatin, and salt; add ⅔ cup water. Stir over low heat till gelatin dissolves; remove from heat. Add cream cheese, yogurt, lemon peel, lemon juice, and food coloring; beat till smooth. Chill till partially thickened. Fold in whipped topping.

To assemble: Place crepe browned side up in greased 2½-inch muffin pan. Spoon about 3 tablespoons cheese filling into crepe; arrange ruffled top. Repeat with remaining crepes. Chill. Before serving, top each with about 1 tablespoon raspberry preserves. Makes 10 servings.

Apple Betty Crepes

½ cup packed brown sugar
⅓ cup all-purpose flour
¼ teaspoon ground cinnamon
⅛ teaspoon ground nutmeg
  Dash salt
¼ cup butter or margarine

2 cups chopped peeled apple
  (2 medium)
2 tablespoons orange juice
8 Feathery Sour Cream Crepes
  (see recipe, page 14)

For topping: Combine brown sugar, flour, cinnamon, nutmeg, and salt. Cut in butter or margarine till mixture is crumbly.

For filling: In bowl toss the chopped apple with orange juice to coat. Combine with ½ cup of the topping mixture.

To assemble: Spoon about ¼ cup of the apple filling along center of unbrowned side of each crepe. Fold two opposite edges of each crepe to overlap atop filling. Place crepes seam side down in 10x6x2-inch baking dish. Sprinkle with remaining topping. Bake at 375° about 25 minutes. Serve warm with ice cream, if desired. Makes 8 servings.

Pear-Sauced Date Crepes

1 *3-ounce package cream cheese,*
   softened
1 *tablespoon milk*
1 *teaspoon sugar*
¼ *teaspoon vanilla*
¼ *cup chopped pitted dates* or
   raisins
¼ *cup chopped walnuts*
1 *16-ounce can pear halves*

2 *tablespoons honey*
1 *tablespoon butter*
4 *teaspoons cornstarch*
½ *cup water*
2 *tablespoons lemon juice*
¼ *teaspoon ground cinnamon*
⅛ *teaspoon ground nutmeg*
12 *Lemon Dessert Crepes (see*
   recipe, page 16)

For filling: In small bowl blend cream cheese, milk, sugar, and vanilla. Stir in dates *or* raisins and walnuts.

For sauce: Drain pears, reserving ¾ cup syrup. Quarter the pear halves; set aside. In skillet or chafing dish heat honey and butter. Blend pear syrup into cornstarch; stir into honey-butter mixture with water, lemon juice, cinnamon, and nutmeg. Cook and stir till thickened.

To assemble: Spread filling over unbrowned side of crepe, leaving ¼-inch rim around edge. Fold in half; fold in half again, forming a triangle. Add crepes and pears to sauce; heat through. Spoon sauce over. Serves 6.

Rhubarb-Strawberry Crepes

2 *egg yolks*
½ *cup sifted powdered sugar*
½ *teaspoon vanilla*
½ *cup whipping cream*
⅔ *cup granulated sugar*

2 *tablespoons cornstarch*
2 *cups sliced rhubarb*
1 *cup sliced strawberries*
12 *Basic Dessert Crepes (see*
   recipe, page 15)

For sauce: Beat together egg yolks, powdered sugar, vanilla, and dash salt till thick and light colored, 3 to 4 minutes. Beat whipping cream till stiff peaks form; fold into yolk mixture. Chill.

For filling: In saucepan stir together granulated sugar and cornstarch; stir in rhubarb, strawberries, and ¼ cup water. Cook and stir till thickened and bubbly. Reduce heat; cook 2 to 3 minutes longer.

To assemble: Spoon about 3 tablespoons filling along center of unbrowned side of crepe. Fold two opposite edges of crepe to overlap atop filling. Place seam side down in 12x7½x2-inch baking dish. Repeat with remaining crepes. Bake, covered, at 375° till heated through, about 15 minutes. Top each serving with chilled sauce. Makes 6 servings.

When dessert time arrives, give *Microwave Cherry Crepes* a try.
Fill the crepes with a spicy cinnamon-yogurt mixture,
add a tasty red cherry sauce, and heat in the microwave oven.

Microwave Cherry Crepes

¾ cup sugar
2 tablespoons cornstarch
2 cups cranberry juice cocktail
1 16-ounce can pitted tart red
  cherries (water pack),
  drained
½ teaspoon grated lemon peel

¼ teaspoon vanilla
  Few drops red food coloring
1 cup yogurt
½ teaspoon ground cinnamon
16 Basic Dessert Crepes (see
  recipe, page 15)

For sauce: In 4-cup glass measure combine ¼ *cup* of the sugar and cornstarch. Stir in cranberry juice, cherries, lemon peel, vanilla, and food coloring. Cook, uncovered, in countertop microwave oven till thickened and bubbly, 5 to 7 minutes, stirring after each minute.
For filling: Combine yogurt, the remaining sugar, and cinnamon.
To assemble: Spread filling over unbrowned side of each crepe, leaving ¼-inch rim around edge. Roll up as for jelly roll. Place seam side down in 12x7½x2-inch baking dish, forming two layers. Spoon sauce over crepes. Micro-cook, covered, about 4 minutes; turn dish once. Serves 8.

Microwave Peanut Butter Crepes

For filling: Blend ½ cup chunk-style peanut butter and ¼ cup honey.
To assemble: Using 12 Whole Wheat Crepes (see recipe, page 14), spread about 1 tablespoon filling over unbrowned side of each crepe, leaving ¼-inch rim around edge. Sprinkle ⅓ cup raisins over crepes. Roll up as for jelly roll. Place seam side down in 12x7½x2-inch glass baking dish. Drizzle 2 tablespoons melted butter over crepes; sprinkle with 2 tablespoons brown sugar. Cook, covered, in countertop microwave oven till hot, about 4 minutes; turn dish once. Makes 6 servings.

Micro-Cooking Crepes

Your countertop microwave oven can perform the same time-saving magic on your crepe recipes as it does on many other dishes. For spur-of-the-moment main dishes or desserts use the microwave oven to prepare the entire recipe as in Microwave Cherry Crepes. Or if you prefer, use the range top to cook the filling and sauce conventionally. Then when the crepes are assembled and placed in a glass baking dish, micro-cook, covered, till heated through, about 4 minutes, turning the dish once.

Orange-Cinnamon Snacks

1 egg white
  Dash cream of tartar
5 Blender Dessert Crepes
  (see recipe, page 14)

¼ cup sugar
1 teaspoon ground cinnamon
1 teaspoon grated orange peel

To assemble: Beat egg white with cream of tartar till stiff peaks form. Spread thinly over unbrowned side of each crepe. Combine sugar, cinnamon, and orange peel; sprinkle over crepes. Cut each in 8 wedges; place on greased baking sheet. Bake at 375° for 10 minutes. Turn oven off; let snacks crisp in closed oven for 20 to 25 minutes. Makes 40 snacks.

Almond-Filled Crepe Cookies

1 8-ounce can almond paste
2 eggs
¾ cup granulated sugar
½ teaspoon vanilla

16 Basic Dessert or Basic Main
    Dish Crepes (see pages 15 or 11)
¾ cup sifted powdered sugar
¼ teaspoon vanilla

For filling: In small bowl break up almond paste. Beat in eggs, granulated sugar, and the ½ teaspoon vanilla till smooth.
To assemble: Spread ¼ cup filling over unbrowned side of each of 8 crepes, leaving ½-inch rim around edge. Top each with another crepe browned side up. Place 4 stacks on ungreased baking sheet. Bake at 375° about 20 minutes. Remove to wire rack. Cool. Repeat with remaining stacks.
For glaze: Mix powdered sugar, ¼ teaspoon vanilla, and dash salt. Blend in 1 tablespoon boiling water till of spreading consistency. Drizzle over stacks. Let glaze harden. Cut stacks in eighths. Makes 64 cookies.

Oriental Fortune Cookies

Write fortunes on paper strips. Mix ¼ cup sifted cake flour, 2 tablespoons sugar, 1 tablespoon cornstarch, and dash salt. Beat in 2 tablespoons cooking oil, 1 egg white, and 1 tablespoon water. Heat a lightly greased 6-inch skillet. Spoon in 1 tablespoon batter; spread with back of spoon to 3½-inch circle. Cook over low heat till lightly browned, about 4 minutes. Turn; cook 1 minute. Remove. Working quickly, place fortune in center; fold in half. Fold again, creasing over edge of a bowl to shape. Set in muffin pan to keep shape; cool. Repeat to make 8.

Pink Squirrel Fondue

1 7-, 9-, or 10-ounce jar
  marshmallow creme
3 tablespoons crème d'almond
1 tablespoon white crème de
  cacao

1 teaspoon lemon juice
• • •
Crepe Chips (see recipe,
  page 16).

In saucepan combine marshmallow creme, crème d'almond, crème de cacoa, and lemon juice. Cook and stir over low heat till heated through, about 2 minutes. Transfer to a small fondue pot; place over fondue burner. Serve Crepe Chips as dippers with fondue. Makes 4 to 6 servings.

Butterscotch Fondue

½ cup butter or margarine
2 cups packed brown sugar
1 cup light corn syrup
1 14-ounce can sweetened
  condensed milk

1 teaspoon vanilla
• • •
Crepe Chips (see recipe,
  page 16)

In saucepan melt butter; stir in sugar, syrup, and 2 tablespoons water. Bring to boiling. Add milk; simmer, stirring constantly, till mixture reaches thread stage (230° on candy thermometer). Add vanilla. Transfer to fondue pot; place over fondue burner. (If mixture becomes thick, add a little milk.) Serve Crepe Chips with fondue. Makes 8 servings.

Elegant Chocolate Fondue

8 1-ounce squares semisweet
  chocolate
1 14-ounce can sweetened
  condensed milk
⅓ cup milk

4 ounces cream-filled mint
  patties, chopped, or 2
  tablespoons instant coffee
  crystals
Crepe Chips (see page 16)

In saucepan melt chocolate; stir in sweetened condensed milk and regular milk till well blended. Cook over low heat till heated through. Stir in mint patties or coffee crystals. Transfer to fondue pot; place over fondue burner. (If mixture becomes thick, stir in a little milk.) Serve Crepe Chips as dippers with fondue. Makes 8 servings.

Flaming specialties

Classic Crêpes Suzette

¼ cup butter or margarine
¼ cup orange liqueur
¼ cup orange juice
3 tablespoons sugar

8 Basic Dessert Crepes
  (see recipe, page 15)
2 tablespoons brandy

For sauce: In skillet or chafing dish combine butter, orange liqueur, orange juice, and sugar; cook and stir till bubbly.

To assemble: Fold a crepe in half, browned side out; fold in half again, forming a triangle. Repeat with remaining crepes; arrange in sauce in skillet or chafing dish. Simmer till sauce thickens slightly, spooning sauce over crepes as they heat. In small saucepan heat the brandy over low heat just till hot. Ignite and pour flaming brandy over crepes and sauce. Makes 4 servings.

Spiced Coffee Crêpes Brûlot

2 3-ounce packages cream
    cheese, softened
¼ cup sifted powdered sugar
2 teaspoons milk
¼ teaspoon finely shredded
    orange peel
  • • •
16 Coffee Dessert Crepes
    (see recipe, page 16)

½ cup granulated sugar
2 tablespoons cornstarch
2 cups cold strong coffee
¼ cup brandy
2 inches stick cinnamon
4 whole cloves
¼ teaspoon finely shredded
    lemon peel
  Chopped nuts (optional)

For filling: Beat cream cheese with powdered sugar, milk, and orange peel till smooth. *Do not chill.*

To assemble: Spread some of the cream cheese filling over unbrowned side of crepe, leaving ¼-inch rim around edge. Roll up crepe as for jelly roll. Repeat with remaining crepes.

For sauce: In saucepan mix together the granulated sugar and cornstarch. Stir in cold coffee. Cook and stir over medium heat till thickened and bubbly; keep warm. In skillet or chafing dish combine brandy, cinnamon, cloves, and lemon peel; heat over low heat just till hot. Ignite brandy mixture. When flame dies, stir in the coffee mixture. Remove cinnamon and cloves; discard. Arrange the filled crepes in coffee sauce; heat through, about 5 minutes, spooning sauce over crepes. Sprinkle with chopped nuts, if desired. Makes 8 servings.

For an impressive ending to a dinner party, serve *Classic Crêpes Suzette*. This traditional dessert flamed with brandy combines crepes folded in quarters with a delicate orange sauce.

Pineapple-Bourbon Crepes

For sauce: Add 2 tablespoons bourbon to one undrained 20-ounce can pineapple slices; let stand overnight. Drain, reserving syrup mixture. Chop fruit; set aside. In saucepan mix ¼ cup sugar, 1 tablespoon cornstarch, ½ teaspoon ground cinnamon, and ½ teaspoon ground nutmeg. Add enough water to reserved syrup to make 1½ cups; blend into sugar mixture. Cook and stir till thickened and bubbly. Stir in 2 tablespoons butter; pour into skillet or chafing dish.

To assemble: Using 12 Basic Dessert Crepes (see recipe, page 15), spoon some chopped pineapple along center of unbrowned side of each crepe. Overlap two opposite edges of each crepe atop filling. Place *seam side up* in sauce. Heat through, spooning sauce over. In small saucepan heat ¼ cup bourbon just till hot. Ignite; pour over crepes. Makes 6 servings.

Raisin-Sauced Crepes

To assemble: Stir ½ cup chopped walnuts into Butterscotch Filling (see recipe, page 19). Using 12 Basic Dessert Crepes (see recipe, page 15), spoon 2 tablespoons filling in center of unbrowned side of each crepe. Fold two opposite edges of each crepe so they overlap atop filling. Fold in other edges of each crepe to form a square packet.

For sauce: Cover ½ cup raisins with boiling water; soak 5 minutes. Drain; reserve ¼ cup liquid. In skillet or chafing dish combine raisins, reserved liquid, ¼ cup brandy, 3 tablespoons brown sugar, ¼ teaspoon grated lemon peel, and 1 tablespoon lemon juice. Bring sauce to boiling. Add crepes; heat through, spooning sauce over. Heat ¼ cup brandy just till hot. Ignite; pour flaming brandy over crepes. Makes 6 servings.

How to Flame Crepes

Serving a flaming crepe dessert is a fitting climax to any special meal. It's easy, too, so give it a try next time you want to impress family or guests. Although any liqueur will flame, for best results, use one that is at least 70 proof. (Liqueur from bottles that have been open for some time may be harder to flame and burn less brightly.) Pour the liqueur into a small saucepan or ladle and heat over low heat or a candle till it starts to vaporize. Then with a long match and keeping clear of the flame, ignite the liqueur and pour it over warm crepes.

Pear-Raspberry Crepes

1 8-ounce carton raspberry
   yogurt
2 tablespoons sugar
16 Blender Dessert Crepes or
   Basic Dessert Crepes (see
   recipes, pages 14 and 15)

1 16-ounce can pear halves
1 10-ounce package frozen
   raspberries, thawed
6 tablespoons orange liqueur
1 tablespoon cornstarch

To assemble: Stir together raspberry yogurt and sugar. Spread about 1 table-spoon yogurt mixture over unbrowned side of crepe, leaving ¼-inch rim around edge. Roll up crepe as for jelly roll. Place on serving platter. Repeat with remaining crepes.

For sauce: Drain pears, reserving ¼ cup syrup. Slice pears; set aside. In blender container combine reserved pear syrup, raspberries, and *2 table-spoons* of the orange liqueur. Cover; blend till smooth. Strain through a sieve. In medium saucepan combine cornstarch with raspberry mixture. Cook and stir till thickened and bubbly. Stir in pears; heat through. In small saucepan heat remaining 4 tablespoons liqueur just till hot; pour into hot sauce. Ignite; pour over crepes. Makes 8 servings.

Banana Crepes Flambé

2 cups chopped banana
   (3 medium to large)
1 tablespoon lemon juice
½ cup toasted shredded coconut
1 teaspoon ground cinnamon
8 Spicy Dessert Crepes
   (see recipe, page 15)

2 tablespoons butter
1 tablespoon light corn syrup
1 package creamy white
   frosting mix (for single
   layer cake)
1 cup evaporated milk
¼ cup rum

For filling: Toss banana with lemon juice to coat. Mix with ¼ *cup* of the shredded coconut and the cinnamon.

To assemble: Spoon ¼ cup filling along center of unbrowned side of each crepe. Fold two opposite edges of each crepe to overlap atop filling.

For sauce: In saucepan cook butter till brown; remove from heat. Stir in corn syrup and about *half* of the frosting mix. Add remaining mix; slowly stir in evaporated milk. Heat through, stirring constantly. Pour into skillet or chafing dish. Add crepes to sauce. Sprinkle with remaining ¼ cup coconut; heat through. Warm rum just till hot. Ignite; pour rum over crepes. Makes 8 servings.

Desserts from afar

Cherry-Topped Cheese Blintzes

1 beaten egg
1 12-ounce carton dry
   cottage cheese (1½ cups)
2 tablespoons sugar
½ teaspoon vanilla
   Dash ground cinnamon

12 Basic Dessert Crepes
   (see recipe, page 15)
2 tablespoons butter
   Canned cherry pie filling,
   heated
   Dairy sour cream

To assemble: Beat together egg, cottage cheese, sugar, vanilla, and cinnamon till nearly smooth. Spoon some cheese mixture in center of unbrowned side of crepe. Fold two opposite edges of crepe to overlap atop filling. Fold in remaining edges, forming a square packet; repeat with remaining crepes. In a skillet cook filled crepes on both sides in butter till heated through. Serve hot crepes with warm cherry pie filling and sour cream. Makes 6 servings.

Italian Apricot Crespelle

¾ teaspoon finely shredded
   orange peel
2 tablespoons orange
   juice
½ recipe Basic Dessert Crepes
   batter (see recipe,
   page 15)
   • • •
½ cup whipping cream
1½ teaspoons sugar

½ teaspoon vanilla
1 16-ounce can unpeeled apricot
   halves
2 tablespoons sugar
   Dash salt
   • • •
1 tablespoon apricot brandy
   or brandy
   Few drops almond extract

For crepes: Stir orange peel and juice into Basic Dessert Crepes batter. Cook as directed for Basic Dessert Crepes, making 10 crepes.
To assemble: Whip cream with 1½ teaspoons sugar and vanilla till soft peaks form. Spread a scant tablespoon cream mixture over unbrowned side of crepes. Fold in half, then in half again, forming a triangle. Repeat with remaining crepes. Cover; refrigerate till ready to serve.
For Apricot Sauce: Drain apricots; reserve ¼ cup syrup. Cut up apricots. In saucepan stir together reserved syrup, apricots, 2 tablespoons sugar, and salt. Simmer, covered, 10 minutes; stir occasionally. Remove from heat; stir in brandy and almond extract. Spoon warm apricot sauce over individual servings of chilled crepes. Makes 5 servings.

A sweetened cottage cheese filling is tucked inside crepes for
Cherry-Topped Cheese Blintzes. If you prefer, serve this
traditional Jewish dessert with jam or sour cream and sugar.

Sundae crepes

Banana Split Crepes

1 *pint strawberry ice cream*
½ *cup crumbled soft coconut*
   macaroons
1 *pint vanilla ice cream*
1 *tablespoon cream sherry*
1 *pint chocolate ice cream*
¼ *cup sliced toasted almonds*
   • • •
8 *small bananas, peeled and*
   halved lengthwise

16 *Basic Dessert Crepes (see*
   recipe, page 15)
Strawberry ice cream topping
Caramel ice cream topping
Pineapple ice cream topping
   • • •
Whipped cream or frozen whipped
   dessert topping, thawed
Strawberries, halved
Chopped walnuts

For ice cream: Several hours before serving, in chilled bowl quickly soften strawberry ice cream; stir in macaroons. Cover; return to freezer immediately. In separate chilled bowl quickly soften vanilla ice cream; stir in sherry. Cover; return to freezer immediately. In third chilled bowl repeat process with chocolate ice cream and almonds.

To assemble: Place a banana half on unbrowned side of each crepe; roll up as for jelly roll. Place two banana rolls seam side down in each of 8 oblong dessert dishes. Top each serving with one small scoop of each of the flavored ice creams. Ladle one of the three ice cream toppings over each scoop of ice cream. Garnish with whipped cream or whipped dessert topping, strawberries, and chopped nuts. Makes 8 servings.

Blueberry-Sauced Crepe Cups

12 *Feathery Sour Cream Crepes*
   (see recipe, page 14)
1 *quart vanilla ice cream*
1 *15-ounce can blueberries*
2 *tablespoons sugar*

1 *tablespoon cornstarch*
⅛ *teaspoon salt*
2 *tablespoons orange*
   liqueur or frozen orange
   juice concentrate, thawed

To assemble: Fit crepes unbrowned side up in 2¾-inch muffin pans. Arrange ruffled tops. Place scoop of ice cream into each. Freeze firm.

For Blueberry Sauce: Drain fruit; reserve syrup. In saucepan combine sugar, cornstarch, and salt; blend in syrup and liqueur or concentrate. Cook and stir till thickened and bubbly. Add fruit; serve warm or chilled.

To serve: Remove crepes from muffin pans. (If necessary, dip pan in warm water for 2 or 3 seconds.) Place crepes on individual dessert dishes. Spoon warm or chilled fruit sauce over. Makes 12 servings.

Take the edge off hot summer days by enjoying *Banana Split Crepes*. This spectacular dessert features easy-to-assemble strawberry-coconut, sherry-vanilla, and chocolate-almond ice creams.

Date-Butter Pecan Crepes

1 *pint butter pecan ice cream*
1⅓ *cups pitted dates, cut up*
1¼ *cups water*
2 *tablespoons sugar*
2 *tablespoons lemon juice*

¼ *teaspoon salt*
¼ *cup chopped toasted pecans*
8 *Blender Dessert Crepes*
   (see recipe, page 14)

For filling: Cut and freeze sticks as directed in tip box.
For Date Sauce: In 2-quart saucepan combine dates, water, sugar, lemon juice, and salt; bring to boiling. Cook and stir over low heat till thickened, about 4 minutes. Fold in pecans; keep warm.
To assemble: Place one frozen stick of ice cream in center of unbrowned side of crepe. Fold two opposite edges of crepe to overlap atop. Place seam side down on dessert dish; repeat with remaining crepes. Spoon warm sauce over. Top with whipped cream, if desired. Makes 8 servings.

Orange and Raspberry Dessert

For filling: Using 1 pint raspberry *or* pineapple sherbet, scoop 30 well-rounded tablespoons and freeze according to tip box directions.
For sauce: In small mixing bowl beat one 3-ounce package cream cheese, softened, and ¼ cup sugar. Fold in one 11-ounce can mandarin orange segments, drained, and one 8-ounce carton lemon yogurt. Cover; chill.
To assemble: Using 10 Fluffy All-Purpose Crepes (see recipe, page 13), place 3 frozen scoops of sherbet in center of unbrowned side of crepe. Fold two opposite edges to overlap atop. Place seam side down on dessert dish; repeat with remaining crepes. Spoon sauce atop. Serves 10.

Chocolate-Banana Crepes

For filling: Cut 1 pint chocolate ice cream into sticks (see tip box).
For sauce: Make one 3⅝- or 3¾-ounce package *instant* vanilla pudding mix by package directions. Fold in 2 sliced bananas. Cover; chill.
To assemble: Using 8 Feathery Sour Cream Crepes (see recipe, page 14), spread about 1 rounded teaspoon creamy peanut butter on unbrowned side of crepe. Center frozen stick of ice cream atop. Fold two opposite edges of crepe to overlap atop. Place seam side down on individual dessert dish; repeat with remaining crepes. Spoon banana-pudding mixture over each. Sprinkle with chopped peanuts, if desired. Makes 8 servings.

Cutting Ice Cream Blocks

The tricky process of filling crepes with ice cream or sherbet becomes easy if you cut the ice cream into sticks. Here's how. *For half gallons:* Open rectangular carton as in drawing below. Cut ice cream in eighths crosswise. Then, cut in quarters lengthwise, making 32 sticks. Place on waxed paper-lined baking sheet so sticks do not touch. Freeze firm. *For pints:* unfold carton as above. Cut ice cream in quarters crosswise. Then in half lengthwise, making 8 sticks. Freeze as above. *If only round cartons are available,* scoop well-rounded tablespoons of ice cream or sherbet on waxed paper-lined baking sheet and freeze. Use 3 of these ice cream scoops to replace one stick.

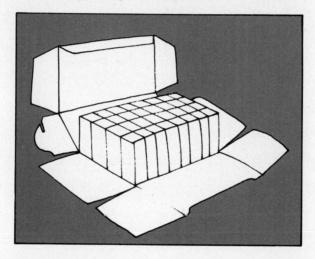

Candied Ginger-Orange Crepes

For filling: Prepare and freeze 1 pint orange sherbet (see tip box).

For Candied Ginger Sauce: In saucepan mix ½ cup sugar, ¼ cup orange-flavored breakfast drink powder, 2 tablespoons finely chopped candied ginger, 2 tablespoons cornstarch, and dash salt. Gradually blend in 1½ cups water. Bring to boiling; cook 2 minutes, stirring constantly. Remove from heat; blend in 2 tablespoons butter *or* margarine. Cool. If desired, cover and refrigerate till ready to assemble crepes.

To assemble: Using 8 Basic Dessert Crepes (see recipe, page 15), place a stick of frozen sherbet in center of unbrowned side of each crepe. Fold two opposite edges of each crepe to overlap atop; place seam side down on dessert dishes. Spoon Candied Ginger Sauce atop each serving. Serves 8.

Mini-Crepes Alaska

½ cup all-purpose flour
¾ cup milk
1 egg
1 tablespoon sugar
1 tablespoon white crème de
   menthe
  Dash salt

1 pint strawberry, vanilla,
   or chocolate ice cream
3 egg whites
½ teaspoon vanilla
¼ teaspoon cream of tartar
⅓ cup sugar

For Crème de Menthe Crepes: In bowl combine the flour, milk, egg, 1 tablespoon sugar, crème de menthe, and salt. Beat with a rotary beater till blended. Heat a lightly greased 6-inch skillet. Remove from heat; spoon in about 2 tablespoons of the batter. Lift and tilt skillet to spread the batter evenly. Return to heat; brown crepe on one side only. *(Or* cook on inverted crepe pan, see page 8.) To remove, invert pan over paper toweling; remove crepe. Repeat with the remaining batter to make 8 crepes, greasing skillet occasionally.

To assemble: Carefully place crepe unbrowned side up in lightly greased 6-ounce custard cup. Spoon about ¼ cup ice cream into crepe. Fold crepe edges down to cover ice cream. Repeat with remaining crepes and ice cream. Freeze till firm. In bowl beat egg whites, vanilla, and cream of tartar till stiff peaks form. Gradually add ⅓ cup sugar, beating till stiff peaks form. Spread meringue over frozen crepe cups, sealing to edges of custard cups. Freeze firm.

To serve: Place frozen custard cups on baking sheet. Bake at 450° till meringue is lightly browned, 4 to 5 minutes. Serve immediately. Serves 8.

Chocolate-Marshmallow Crepes

½ cup tiny marshmallows
  Chocolate Filling
   (see recipe, page 19)

12 Chocolate Dessert Crepes
   (see recipe, page 15)
  Vanilla ice cream

For filling: Stir marshmallows into chilled Chocolate Filling.

To assemble: Spoon about three tablespoons filling in center of unbrowned side of crepe. Fold two opposite edges of crepe so they overlap atop filling. Fold in remaining edges, forming a square packet. Place seam side down in dessert dish; repeat with remaining crepes. Top each with a small scoop of ice cream. Sprinkle with chocolate shavings, chopped nuts, *or* toasted coconut, if desired. Makes 12 servings.

Index

index

index